Wholeness
Within

Wholeness *Within*

Insights from One Woman's Journey of
Creating a Life and Career in Alignment

EMILY SMITH

GUIDE *to*
WHOLENESS

Published by Guide to Wholeness, Reading, MA
www.guidetowholeness.com

Edited and designed by Girl Friday Productions
www.girlfridayproductions.com

Cover design: Kathleen Lynch
Interior design: Paul Barrett
Project management: Reshma Kooner and Laura Dailey
Image credits: All photos courtesy of the author. Cover and
interior circle motif © Getty Images/Anna Erastova

ISBN (paperback): 979-8-9853630-0-5
ISBN (ebook): 979-8-9853630-1-2

CONTENTS

INTRODUCTION

To live is the rarest thing in the world. Most
people exist, that is all.

—Oscar Wilde

I started each workday on the subway, packed against fellow
riders. Grand Central station was ten minutes from my apartment, and as I walked, I felt quite small against the backdrop
of the skyscrapers. When I got off the subway at Fulton Street,
the damp smell of sewer waste, mixed with seawater, met me.
It was not a pleasant smell first thing in the morning, especially on hot summer days. I should have remembered this
when I first smelled it on the morning of my day-long interview
for the job. As well as the smells of hot trash radiating off the
sidewalk on ninety-degree days combined with body odor in a
tightly packed subway car with malfunctioning AC. As someone sensitive to fragrances and odors, I found New York City
could quickly make me nauseous if I wasn't careful.

Another ten-minute walk brought me to my office in the
Seaport district, right on the banks of the East River, at the
southernmost tip of Manhattan. At least five security guards,
including some police officers, guarded the entrance on most
days. I flashed my badge to access the elevator port.

My sun-drenched office was on the fifteenth floor. Glass windows looked out over the pier, where the outside world looked idyllic. Ships cruising by, tourists walking along the water, a sun-drenched reprieve so different from the environment inside the concrete jungle. Inside, the office bustled with my coworkers, and because many of them were from my university and my team back in Boston, I already had connections before I started. I often worked in conference rooms with friends, took walks with them along the East River on our breaks, and went out with them after work to the bar at the back of the building, where the bartender charged us only fifty cents a drink because we were regulars.

I was living my (so-called) dream life in the city, sharing an ornate, modern Midtown apartment with friendly roommates and working in a prestigious job in Manhattan. These things were supposed to make me happy and powerful, but they didn't. In fact, I felt just the opposite. I hadn't looked deep enough within myself when I'd made my decision to move to New York, two years after graduating university. I knew it would look good on my résumé and that it was a stimulating place where people who "made it" went.

I used my social life as a distraction from my unhappiness. Alcohol was the numbing agent, the glue that brought people together who normally wouldn't commune. With plenty of office social events, there were myriad opportunities to distract myself in the buzz of social connection. But after less than two years as an account executive, the work no longer felt meaningful. I began to just go through the motions of a role because I thought that was the only path laid out for me. I clung to my job and lifestyle, for safety, afraid of the unknown where I would have to carve my own path and support myself financially in a new career. Plus, I had student loans I couldn't default on, believing that I would be "sent to jail" if I did so. At least, that was what my mom had told me, and I felt that fear on a visceral level. The pressure of having to pay $1,000 a month for my student loan bill was enough to make me take any job that would look good, even great, on my résumé, and above all else, a job that would ensure my financial needs were met. As each workday passed, it became increasingly clear that corporate culture wasn't for me, even though I so desperately wanted it to be. I thought that being a successful corporate worker was my entire identity—it was who I was *supposed* to be. I had been praised for it, and for the first time in my life, I had felt seen and appreciated for my work. That feeling boosted my ego.

My patience with myself, and my career, was starting to wear thinner and thinner. I had already lived in London (just a year prior) in search of myself, chasing success, and that had certainly been a growth experience—moving far away from home, taking on a new job, and even speaking up for myself about being bullied and about not having sufficient resources to do my job. But I had gotten fired the next day. *Just before my birthday.* For someone who had identified self-worth with external achievements, being fired felt, with no exaggeration, like I was being killed. In an emotional sense, I was. And getting sacked on my birthday, no less, felt deeply personal.

But when I returned to America, I held on to the same corporate career path because I didn't see an alternate one—this was all I knew. I also held on to the pain from my experience in London, and I found it hard to trust my decisions. I wound up repeating similar painful experiences in new roles at new companies.

How did I get to this point of playing out a cycle that clearly wasn't working? Because I kept trying the same strategy without getting new results, going back to what I knew. I placed my entire sense of self-worth outside myself. I lived like a victim. But this warped perspective of myself was not sustainable when everything I had built my worth on crumbled. I began to see myself as broken, as unworthy. I spiraled deeper and deeper into a dark abyss of self-loathing. And then something happened that would change my life forever. After that portal opened, I began to see that failure is necessary to move forward, and I began to discover how to dig my way out of the pit and set myself on a path toward spiritual awakening.

I'd never felt like I fit in anywhere while growing up in a suburb twenty minutes north of Boston. Being a first-generation child, with parents from France and Scotland, I carried that "outsider" mentality with me no matter where I was. I was different: I felt my experiences on a deep level, and I was highly creative. I viewed the world a little differently from my peers. But as a kid, I just wanted to be the same as them. To fit in and be accepted. I spent most of my life trying to fit myself into a box until I eventually succeeded in that goal. When I did that, though, I came face-to-face with the stark realization that I didn't know who I was. With no other choice, I had to finally show up as the real me, however terrifying that seemed.

Many of the lessons I share in this book are universal, including the truth that in order to learn to see my own worth I had to integrate the aspects of myself that I didn't like. In these pages, I detail my own experiences and how my newfound spiritual approach to life helped me overcome the challenges I faced, which once seemed insurmountable. I also share how a variety of tools, including dream interpretation, essential oils, breathwork, meditation, and journaling, helped me uncover ancestral patterns, heal trauma, trust and embody my authentic self, and rewrite my story. I describe how I turned around and started helping others by becoming certified as an integrative life coach, an essential oils specialist, and a breathwork facilitator. I developed a curriculum for a one-to-one spiritual coaching program, which has helped women in their thirties who feel unfulfilled and stuck to learn how to feel fulfilled, whole, and connected to their work while navigating major life transitions. Some of their stories are included in these pages, and their names have been changed to protect privacy.

I've found that writing is a way to share wisdom with others, through my blog on Guide to Wholeness (www.guideto wholeness.com), through my Medium page of the same name, on Thought Catalog under "Emily Smith," and on my LinkedIn page (www.linkedin.com/in/emilymsmith1/). In 2018, while at a workshop on memoir writing, I received a clear message from my higher self that I would be writing this book you're reading today.

My hope is that by seeking and accepting support from the universe and by using the tools I describe in these pages, you also will learn to feel secure in who you are, heal your past, and find your soul's work. That you will fully accept yourself as you are, trust yourself to make the right decisions, and cultivate the life you desire through your mindset and conscious creation. Know that you are not alone, and that even though this journey of awakening can feel like a transition that will never end, so much is waiting for you on the other side of meeting and understanding your pain. Whenever you resonate with what I share, be sure to share your takeaway and how it affected you: use the book's hashtag, #wholenesswithin, and on Instagram tag @guidetowholeness.

Let me now take you a few steps back, to where this journey began for me.

PART 1

Walking Open Wound

CHAPTER 1

The Matrix

Your own Self-Realization is the greatest service you can render the world.

—Ramana Maharshi

You've probably heard the term the "matrix." A matrix is essen-
tially a program. When you follow a program, you don't really
choose the life you want to lead, even if, on the surface, it *looks*
like you do. As a human living in our world today, it's inevitable
to be influenced by the outside world and its societal "rules."
A typical matrix program is one that says the key to success
looks like this: get accepted into an Ivy League university,
land a successful career, get married, have kids, buy a house,
retire, finally live the life you truly want, and then die. This
"prescribed path" sticks out in the matrix; it's a clearly laid-out
program to follow. I knew as a student in university that I did
not want to be working in a cubicle, "working for the man,"
until I died. I already had had a taste of this type of lifestyle
during my internships throughout university. I interned in all

different types of industries: at a small wealth-planning office, a global marketing department in a tech robotic company, and an insurance corporation. I spent most of my time supporting busy life insurance agents, financial planners, or marketing managers who gave me typical administrative tasks that I would usually complete in the first hour of being at the office. I yearned for more, but I didn't get it.

I would dread heading to work, because I would be bored out of my mind there: filing papers, updating spreadsheets, scrolling Facebook on my phone, counting down the hours, and wishing I were somewhere else. I would even make sure that I wasn't *one minute* too early by staying in my car as long as I could, playing on my phone until 8:59 a.m., when I would begrudgingly head inside. I couldn't understand how most of society lived this way. I saw no one I knew that was in work they were passionate about, something else you don't see in the matrix. Yet it was the exact path I was on. It was all I knew.

Once I started working full-time in the corporate world, I came face-to-face with this path that I had seen coming—the prescribed path of the matrix. Eventually I realized I had to take my destiny into my own hands and step out of this program. I started dreaming about my escape. This trajectory had all been temporary in my mind. I was *supposed* to get an internship *so that* I could land a full-time job right out of university. Everything I had been working so hard for was leading up to this. But I wanted to lead a life of travel, freedom, and fulfillment, so I set out to create that for myself.

If you've read the acclaimed book *The Secret* by Rhonda Byrne, you know that Byrne talks about how to design a life of luxury by using manifestation techniques to attract money and other desired outcomes for your life. I'd read the book when I was in high school, and even at that age I was influenced by the lesson taught—that you have the power to create your reality. Once I'd landed in the corporate world and realized that I needed to make a change, I did whatever I could to manifest that reality and turned back to the book I had read years ago. Although I wasn't far enough along in my personal growth journey in 2014, just a year after graduating university, I instinctively knew I needed to manifest some sort of change in my life. It was up to me to make this happen. I decided I wanted to live abroad and work in London—this was how I was going to start living my life on *my* terms. London seemed so foreign and glamorous to me. It was English speaking, so I figured it would be easy enough to jump right in and adjust, without having the challenge of a language barrier. This was after I had started my career in Boston at a global marketing agency I'll call Artel.

Reading the book The Secret *while on vacation in Florida during my junior year of high school. A friend had let me borrow it. I became obsessed with the idea that our thoughts create our reality, and since I loved the book so much, my friend let me keep it.*

There were a number of reasons why I wanted to live in London. It was where my friends in university had done an internship one summer, and they had loved it. I heard their stories of clubbing at world-famous places like Fabric and the Ministry of Sound, trying out the delicacies at Borough Market and Ben's Cookies, and going to Wimbledon and the Tower of London. I had to experience it for myself. I had been to London a handful of times while growing up, but only for a weekend or day trip. (Pro tip: Don't move somewhere you haven't spent time in for a long term.) My desire to move there, though, was likely related to a pattern passed down to me by my dad. He had decided he wanted to move to America to be successful in his career, by emigrating from Scotland, at the exact same age I was when contemplating this move. Uncanny, right? It's no secret we pick up on our parents' programming too.

My entire being was set on making this "dream life" of mine happen, because I saw this as the only way to exit the miserable, predictable matrix of pushing papers at my job in Boston. I was well aware that I was working in a reputable company where I was being trained and given professional opportunities, but I still felt empty. I had graduated with a marketing degree, expecting a creatively inspired career path like fashion marketing. I had had a successful first year: I had earned a promotion, been able to travel to New York City for client meetings, and enjoyed the people I worked with. No matter how much I tried, I just couldn't get excited about the type of work I was doing, which was centered around data management. So, I got busy making this vision of escaping the matrix my reality. And what I did create was a miracle; our thoughts and intentions truly *do* create our realities. But I was basing my decision to move on a pattern that was not my own and on a superficial goal. I would not realize either of these truths until further down the line.

Meeting DJ John O'Callaghan at the Ministry of Sound in London, while riding on someone's shoulders. It felt surreal to meet him because the first time I had seen him play was in the summer of 2013 at this exact club, which was an experience that, only a year later, had factored into my decision to move to London.

Even as a young adult, I had wanted to live and travel abroad, and I believe that had to do with my upbringing by European parents. I traveled every summer to visit my grandparents in France and Scotland, so the love of travel was cultivated in me at a young age. My first flight alone was at the age of eight, and situations like that started to bring me out of my shell. Until my parents sent me on that cross-Atlantic flight, I had been painfully shy, uncomfortable around other people. My worst fear about that flight wasn't changing terminals or finding my gate, *it was having to sit next to someone I didn't know.* But necessity cultivates growth, and I quickly discovered that young children traveling alone attract all sorts of attention from flight attendants and fellow travelers. I reveled in delight from all these caring souls, making new friends, and at some level, I came to believe that travel meant human connection.

As I got older, my love of travel only grew, along with the desire to know my heritage. Because both my parents are immigrants, we didn't celebrate Thanksgiving as a family; instead, we made trips to Montreal and Quebec every November. And frankly I still don't feel connected at all to what that holiday was based on. There, I felt as if I was more a citizen of the world than a citizen of either America or Europe. And I wanted to know more about the European aspect of my lineage, perhaps to find a degree of wholeness in myself that felt missing even in my youth, as I did my best to integrate into North American culture.

In my junior year of university, I studied abroad in Florence, Italy, where I truly got my first taste of independence and where my insatiable thirst for travel was quenched for a short time. Everyone in the study-abroad program referred to it as a six-month vacation, but for me, every day was filled with new experiences and challenges. And when I was able to face and overcome those challenges, I felt empowered. Finding my way to class through the streets of Florence without a map for the first time, speaking only in Italian to my home-stay hosts, and navigating trips on my own to other European cities, like Prague, showed me I was capable of more than I had ever been aware of.

At Piazzale Michelangelo during my first week in Firenze (Florence), Italy, in 2011. It was in Firenze that I first connected with the carefree aspect of myself—the version of myself on vacation, living la dolce vita and enjoying the freedom of living abroad as a student.

By moving to London, I was trying to get that part of my life back, when I had felt so free and self-assured, starting each

day curious and inspired by my surroundings. I didn't realize
how different *working* in London would be from being a young
adult at university traveling abroad. All I knew was that I had
this compulsion to move to London; in fact, proving to myself
that I could do this was more important than even the actual
experience of being there. I was going to prove to everyone that
I could do it. I seemingly had everything going for me in my
marketing career and life at home, with many new friends and
a romantic partner. But I proceeded forward with the plan to
move anyway, because of this insatiable desire, which uprooted
my entire life and led me to the unknown. A path that was outside the matrix and was instead an enviable lifestyle—at least,
that's what I believed it to be.

After my first year at Artel, where I worked in their program for new graduates, I asked about the possibility of transferring to one of their offices in Europe. I had an account
management role, where I supported clients in managing their
projects and the finances associated with them as I acted as a
liaison between the different technical groups involved. Early
on, I learned essential business acumen and client relationship
management skills. In just my third month of work, I had traveled to New York City with my team for the day to sit in on the
quarterly business review of client accounts. I was even given
the opportunity to help present some of the data to our clients.

I had my first taste of personal and professional development when I took part in a company training for the new
grads, based on *The 7 Habits of Highly Effective People* by
Stephen R. Covey, which gave me insight into how to manage
myself as an executive. I also learned much about high performance from my managers, who were all at the vice president
level or above. But I wanted to be using my creativity more
and to move closer to the marketing aspect of the role versus
the client relationship management. There wasn't a creative
marketing group at the Massachusetts office, which focused

more on database marketing, but I learned there were creative agencies in the company's European offices. When I asked HR about transferring abroad, at the advice of my manager, I was told that international transfers were only for senior people in the company. Rather than this response serving as a sign to give up, it only made me want it more. When someone tells me I can't do something, it can often prompt me to dig deeper and desire it more.

When clients were giving her pushback and attitude, my first manager, Kelly, frequently (and I quickly learned, sarcastically) would say, "I love my job, I love my job, I love my job." Even then, it felt so wrong to me to live a life I had to *pretend* I loved. I had to take a risk to find what I was yearning for.

Although my career seemed ideal on the surface, I had by now come to view it as the doom-and-gloom, nine-to-five lifestyle. Transitioning to this work schedule out of university, where my classes hadn't started until after noon and I had no responsibilities but to pass classes, had been soul crushing. I wasn't working on the shiny marketing projects I'd been expecting, and I was living in my mom's basement to save money. London could be my ticket out of there! Even after being told that a transfer wasn't an option for me yet, I continued to obsessively check the company's intranet job site and to visualize the job I wanted: an account executive role like the one I currently held but in a creative agency and posted in London. I was *certain* this move would make my life better. How could it not?

The director of HR connected me with the UK recruiting manager at my company, even though no jobs were currently available for me, and we talked on the phone and then over email about why I wanted to transfer to London. I believe Andrew, the recruiter, could tell I was only seeing the best parts and what I *wanted* to see, and he mentioned in an email that he, likewise, had moved to Maryland from the UK in search of something new and more satisfying. But he'd then moved back home.

"Sometimes we think the grass is greener on the other side," he wrote.

I let that clue pass right over me and thought self-righteously, *Well, that's just his experience, and not mine.* I was still certain I wanted to live like a European. I desired their five-weeks-plus vacation policies and laid-back lifestyles, as well as the concept of jetting off to see a new country each weekend. I was enamored by Europe's fashion and its nightlife too. It would be a stark contrast to the American culture I knew, which I felt was so centered on the daily grind at work. That's exactly what I was trying to escape from.

Riding on the top floor of a double-decker bus in Edinburgh, Scotland. I was born in that city, and I lived on the Royal Mile for the first year of my life. While I was growing up in Stoneham, my family visited Edinburgh once a year. I have a deep connection with this place.

One month later, I got an email from the recruiter. A new job had appeared, seemingly out of nowhere! A new team was created in central London, and they would be working on-site with the client, instead of at the office. The client was a prestigious company I'll call Cartra, and I could hardly believe what I was reading. This was so much better than I'd ever imagined! Cartra would be *my* client, and their office would be *my* office, every day. I looked up the address online and saw pictures of its stunning architecture. It was located near high-end shops and decorative streetlights dotted with crystal globes. Its expansive rooftop deck, with a lawn and patio furniture, was facing a giant glittering wall with a design of the Union Jack.

I would be working with *Cartra*, directly supporting their team on their own campus. *Who in their right mind would say no to that?* This company represented a true marker of external success in society, with the building's unique orange exterior, the juice bars, and the daily chef-made meals. It also represented the opposite of my current company culture at Artel in the US. Cartra was hip, while the Artel office was traditional. As I continued to follow the instructions from *The Secret*, I visualized walking onto the plane at the airport and feeling so proud, all dressed up in a pantsuit; I imagined that people would think, *She's a powerful badass!* I allowed this feeling to sink in deep: I saw myself walking into the office, spending time on the gorgeous rooftop patio, and going on runs along the river Thames each day.

This was the opportunity of a lifetime. I didn't need to hear any more details. My ego was driving the show, and it already had everything it needed to make this decision. Cartra was an automatic *yes*. My job offer came via email, and as I read the message, a surge of dopamine rushed and took over my entire body. In this role, I was also offered a promotion to senior account executive.

I raced to the bathroom and sat in a stall in absolute awe, running my hands through my hair. *I am going to London, to work on-site at Cartra!* I had achieved what I had set out to do. I had made things happen in my physical reality by using my intentions.

Before I left for London, my manager at the time, Ron, gave me a book called *The Four Agreements* by Don Miguel Ruiz. This manager had made a positive impact on me, demonstrating what a great leader embodies and giving me autonomy to do my best job. Ron mentioned that he wasn't religious at all but that this spiritual book had helped him in his life and he was giving it to me as a gift. With this comment, I considered for the first time how spirituality can be different from religion. This book was a tool eerily similar to *The Secret*, in that it taught you to be mindful of your thoughts, but for a purpose other than material success: *its purpose was for inner peace*. It was a small whisper of truth that momentarily interrupted my ego's voice with an invitation to begin addressing my heart's needs, not my ego's. The timing of this gift was uncanny, as I was about to enter a period in my life when this book's messages would have truly helped me.

But my ego's desires were too loud, and they drowned out the book's true message. London and Cartra's campus were luring me with their casual culture and promises of opportunity, which fueled my sense of self. I had no idea of the darkness I was about to step into.

CHAPTER 2

London

Only those who dare to fail greatly can ever
achieve greatly.

—Robert F. Kennedy

Moving to London was one of the hardest things I'd done
in my life. At age twenty-three, I was young and naive, and
despite being an experienced traveler and having lived over-
seas for six months while studying in Florence, I had never
truly lived, *or worked* for that matter, on my own, in another
country. This was a whole new ball game, and I was playing in
the big leagues, career-wise. I seriously underestimated what I
was doing.

The move started with me almost missing my flight. I was
having dinner at Logan airport with my partner at the time,
and we didn't want to say goodbye. This was the last possible place before security where we could be together. As we
sipped on pink guava cocktails, holding hands, my partner,
Asif, repeated over and over how much he would miss me.

How much he loved me. I was suddenly torn. I had craved this external show of love and affection so much, perhaps more than my partner himself. Now I was enjoying being lavished with attention, and I was going to leave this source of validation to follow my dreams. Which were just another form of validation. Asif made it clear he wanted to spend every last possible minute with me before I left, and without setting any boundary, I obliged.

"Emily Smith, your plane is now boarding. Please proceed to your gate. This is the final boarding call."

As I heard the announcement, I wondered, *Is this really happening?* After a tearful goodbye, I raced to the gate to make my flight. Instead of calmly boarding the plane as the pantsuit-wearing badass, as in my visualization, I was an out-of-breath, disheveled, and teary traveler heading into the unknown as I trotted down the jetway.

Once I arrived in London, I became immediately aware of the cultural differences, something I wasn't expecting. I came to the realization that I *was* American. Most of my life, I had considered myself to be more French or more Scottish, especially as I had been born in Scotland. But I'd spent over twenty years in the US and only got my American citizenship right before moving to London, so that I could live there permanently with dual citizenship. This was symbolic, as I had to leave the US to realize that I identified with its culture more than with my European roots. But citizenship was only one way that I would feel like an outsider.

In front of Faneuil Hall Marketplace in Boston after getting my US citizenship at the Great Hall. I was so excited and ready to embark on my journey to London.

I had been an introvert growing up, and would go to different soccer camps every summer with my best friend, Anna, who was very extroverted. Every time, she would effortlessly connect with so many new friends, and people were instantly drawn to her because she was so open and outgoing. Me, on the other hand? I felt shy and uncomfortable, and I would have been happy just being with her, the two of us. At the same time, I *wished* I could be as outgoing and confident as her, but it just didn't feel like a possibility for me. I was scared. Now here I was in London, and although I'd been to Europe many times as a child and still had some relatives in the UK and Spain, I felt completely alone when I arrived. Not knowing anyone in the city felt like going off to summer camp again, but this time without my extroverted friend to help. I was forced to be outgoing and reach out to others. I would not be able to wait for others to come to me.

This was extremely uncomfortable and lonely. I didn't like to be seen, because there were parts of myself that I was ashamed of and thought others wouldn't like to see. When I had leukemia as a three-year-old, I would catch side-glances from others, staring at my bald head, and I knew that I was different from them. I couldn't stand it, and I internalized that shame. At that point, my role models were Disney princesses with hair that flowed down their backs, and yet I didn't have any hair at all. What did that say about me? Well, I concluded that it meant something must have been wrong with me. As a child, I was going through an experience that I felt no one else understood. The stress of frequent hospital visits contributed to the loss of that carefree essence that you naturally have as a child. I grew up quickly from that experience and carried the weight of the shame of being *different* with me. But now I could no longer hide. I was in a senior-level position, and would have to be fully seen. I would have to come out from the shadows and show myself, even if I was shaking and wary. The pressure to succeed was almost too much to bear, which didn't help.

I also had to advocate for myself. I had to put effort into making connections, finding an apartment, signing up for health insurance, opening a bank account, getting a phone card, and accomplishing a million other tasks that come with moving to a new country that I hadn't thought through. I don't recommend winging it when moving, by the way. Because I hadn't prepared enough before leaving, I didn't understand the layout of the city and chose to temporarily stay in Airbnb rentals, all spread out from each other in the huge city, until I could find an apartment. I didn't know which neighborhoods were safe or in my budget, and I even haphazardly packed my suitcase the night before I moved (*yikes*). I found that I was missing a lot of items that I needed upon arrival, including an umbrella because it was now October, the rainy season, in London. I also didn't understand cultural norms or expressions, save for a few, and found myself lost in conversations over the simplest things, like not understanding that "takeaway" meant "to go" when leaving with leftovers from a restaurant. The British accent would confuse me, and I was frustrated that I couldn't even understand it. Sometimes the hardest experiences you go through give you the knowledge and wisdom you need. I learned an important lesson—to always be prepared when you can. Today I know how much better and more confident I am when I'm prepared.

Beyond the administrative tasks of life, I was also faced with social challenges I hadn't anticipated. To an observer, my life may have appeared exciting and luxurious: meeting colleagues from all over the world, attending outings for the new team in upscale restaurants and hotel bars, enjoying gourmet food service at Cartra's campus, and celebrating holidays and other events through extravagant parties and gift exchanges. But on the inside, I was falling into a dark depression.

I had difficulty even talking and expressing myself. It's hard to explain, but I felt like I was outside my body. When I would try to say something—to a new colleague, for example— I would find myself shutting down, for fear of rejection. It was much easier to hide myself than to risk being rejected. It felt

like it took too much energy to express myself, so I put on a
mask. But when I shut down, I came off as "cold," aloof even.
It was as if I had left my old, true self back in Boston, and this
new self was just an empty shell. I had only known myself by
seeing how people I knew perceived me at home. I felt a deep
sense of loneliness that I couldn't shake, even though I was surrounded by people.

My mind went to dark places in this out-of-body experience. I had depressing thoughts about life in general, and irri-
table feelings toward myself and others. To avoid this deeply
uncomfortable pain, I turned to the two things I knew would
numb me: alcohol and my romantic relationship with Asif
back in the US. It's possible to use people as drugs. I was far too
dependent on Asif, because he was a familiar, constant source
of approval and support. It was harder to be independent and
do the work to fully engage and embrace my experience, so I
clung to my relationship for safety. Constant WhatsApp messages and nightly FaceTime calls, when we'd both fall asleep
together, were my lifelines. I leaned on my partner to avoid that
feeling of being alone.

This downward shift in my mood was such a strange and
novel sensation for me that I didn't even recognize something
was wrong. I thought I just had to push through the stress
and pain, and I didn't address my emotions. That's what I'd
been taught to do when I was growing up. But I was facing
culture shock, and even though I'd taken a class on culture
shock before studying abroad in Italy, I wasn't prepared for
the real thing this time. It's an overwhelming and disorienting
phenomenon that, when combined with moving, can be one of
life's most stressful trials.

As the months went by, I had some visitors. Two of my
best friends from home traveled to be with me, bringing their
partners. Asif came along, too, and together we all explored
London and toured the Canary Islands. I met up with a family

friend, Kathy, at her home in Norfolk, England. I visited my godfather in Scotland and another family friend who was studying abroad in Edinburgh. I also traveled to Spain to visit my younger sister, Lara, who was studying abroad there. At the time, we were close, with our friend groups enmeshed. We all loved to party and drink together.

But even with all these connections, I felt despair, because all that I'd done over the course of the past year to realize this dream wasn't making me feel fulfilled after all. I was disconnected from myself, as if I were living a stranger's life. It was a deeply unsettling feeling, realizing that I didn't know who I was *at all*, because the life I thought I desired left me feeling so empty. When I visited my sister in Spain, I experienced my first nervous breakdown unexpectedly, during a night out drinking, as I came to terms with the fact that I was in way over my head. I remember uncontrollably crying in the bathroom and gasping for breath on the cab ride home. Every emotion I had stuffed down came up when I was under the influence and with someone I felt safe with.

I was depressed. And disappointed. I had put so much faith and effort into this mission of mine, and three months into the move I discovered it was not what I wanted. I had zero compassion toward myself, and my inner-critic voice had taken over completely. This hadn't been a decision led by my heart, as much as I'd believed it was. It was a decision led by my ego, influenced by societal programming, which said moving to a European city and working for a prestigious company were the keys to success and happiness.

Once I was in London, I didn't understand British culture, which felt cold and unexpressive to me. While I was used to warm and kind family members from Britain, the city culture wasn't emotionally expressive; it was more subdued. Coming from the US, where I found everyone, for the most part, to be outwardly friendly (and very loud), it was a stark contrast that

I didn't expect would affect me as much as it did. London felt quiet, almost withdrawn to me, and I took it personally. I felt invisible, and it heightened my sense of loneliness. At work, any jokes about me being American put me on edge. The first thing my manager said in the elevator as we headed up on my first day was, "You're no longer in Disneyland, like America." *What?* He meant that people take things seriously in the U.K., that this is how the "real world" operates. I now understand making repeated comments about someone's nationality and country of origin is a form of harassment. I was still the misfit.

The food also wasn't what I was used to, and I missed the healthy routines and comfort foods I had at home. English buildings seemed much smaller, and the lack of space affected my well-being. The air quality wasn't great, and it rained every single day for a month when I first arrived. When I blew my nose, black snot appeared on the tissue.

My German roommate, Kira, who worked in fashion at Burberry's corporate office, laughed. "Get used to this in London." Later, she would find a huge growth of mold on the wall in her room, which our landlord never took care of.

The city was spread out, much larger than it appeared on a map, and the street address formats were so confusing. I got lost everywhere I went through the old streets, even when using my Maps app. I typically would arrive at my destination at least twenty minutes late. Sometimes I never found my destination at all and had to return to my apartment disheartened.

Finding a place to live when I arrived, while working full-time, wore me down. For nearly two months, I moved from one Airbnb to another because there were no long-term stays available at that time. And each time I lugged my life in a suit-case down cobbled streets, I felt a little more depleted. I stayed in Camden when I first arrived, sleeping on a daybed, where the host would make me delicious vegan meals that I missed greatly when I left. The second stay was in a home in North

London, followed by a home in Marylebone, then Tooting, and then Mitcham. Finally, after five Airbnb rentals, I took one of the first apartments I saw in a viewing, because it had been so hard to even schedule the appointments while I was at my new job. I picked this place even though my room was going to be an office that had been converted into a bedroom, with this kitschy white-and-black-patterned wallpaper, which I thought was endearing—until I realized that if I looked at the wall too long, it made me dizzy as it swirled in my line of vision like a kaleidoscope. The room was so tiny that, when lying down on my single bed, I could touch the walls on either side with my hands. I also had five roommates—yes, five—in the apartment. There was no living room, only a kitchen area to escape the Harry Potter closet of a room that I was staying in.

Depression hit me like a tidal wave the first week after I moved into the new place, but I tried to hide it. I had stayed with a friend of my French family, Clara, for the first few days in London, as her apartment was close to Heathrow airport, and it was clear right away that Clara wasn't enjoying living in London. She complained about how everything was so expensive, how it rained too much, how her roommate didn't do her share of cleaning, and how far she had to travel to get to her job in central London. Not exactly the first experience you want to have when you move somewhere new. I didn't give myself any time to wallow, though, because I had to train my entire focus on my new job.

I believe every place has an energetic imprint—a resonance—and a medicine for you. Although my energy didn't match that of London's, the place offered the medicine I needed. It taught me to be understanding of people I didn't understand. Most importantly, it took me out of the bubble I'd been in. Now that I was in London, I had to grow up quickly and be truly responsible for myself, and my life, for the first time. This is what I had told everyone I would do, and I saw going back home as a failure. *Besides, who the hell would walk away from Cartra?* So I stayed, begrudgingly.

Although getting acquainted with London, and becoming settled in my apartment, contributed to my culture shock and despair, my life at work was even more debilitating. My entire team was new, with about ten of us starting on the same day and just a couple of "original" people, who had started only months prior, to train us. There were no processes in place, no onboarding system. I sat at a table with all these other people, with no dividers or cubicles, just a mere foot apart, and they were from Cartra, not from my own company. It was an awkward dynamic, where I felt I didn't truly belong, even if it looked like it from the outside. It was clear to me that only those with elevated status were the *real* Cartra employees.

As it was all new, there was no process documentation, and this was the first time I realized I thrive with structures in place. The two team members who had been there longer, by six months, were not overly helpful, and the ten of us needed to try to figure out things together, but it was tough. To top it off, I had a Mac computer when I was used to a PC, so I had that learning curve as well. And my role was entirely new, with new responsibilities. In short, it was challenging because there were so many changes at once.

Office politics were the name of the game here, but that was not the culture I had come from at the office in Boston. Here, lying was the norm, as long as it made you look good. I quickly learned that how you were *perceived* by colleagues, or how you sold yourself, mattered more than what you actually produced: it was all about the illusion of being a high performer. It was clear that employees also received more professional opportunities if they had a close, even personal, relationship with people in leadership. It seemed to me that your performance didn't matter; what mattered was that you were favored by the account director and managers. And if you weren't friends with those two people who had a few months of history on the account, then they wouldn't help you with any questions you had. I learned, albeit in this extreme way, that relationships matter in your career just as much as your performance does. You could be a top performer, but if you don't take the time to get to know the people you work with as much as you do the work itself, you won't have a solid working relationship to get support or to help you look forward to coming in to work.

I didn't play this game, though; until that point, I had been promoted solely based on professional merit, which had also been the basis of my positive work relationships. In London it was different, and it didn't help that I wasn't a good fit for this new role. Even if I had wanted to try, I couldn't pretend to make it work. I knew from the start that there were going to be problems. I couldn't imagine then how bad it could get.

Going from a traditional cubicle office, as I'd had in my job in Boston, to a brightly colored, fantasy office was another type of culture shock. I thought an environment with whimsical-patterned wallpaper would inspire me creatively and get me out of the matrix with its gray cubicle walls. Instead, all it gave me was more anxiety. Was this a place in which to play or to work? My brain couldn't decide. Even though there were authentic coffee makers with espresso like you see in Italian coffee shops and all the snacks you could help yourself to, plus napping pods and daily yoga classes on-site, I didn't do my best work there. I soon realized that I'd stepped into a place that expects your work to constitute your entire life. Working there was intended to be your identity.

I went in early for breakfast, as some of my colleagues did, and would get poached eggs with salmon on toast and would make carrot and apple juice at the juice bar. After work, I would either eat dinner in the same cafeteria or bring something home from there to eat, to save money. This was a slippery slope, where personal life and work life became one, in a sneaky way. My personal life became dependent on my work life. It was clear everyone knew they had made it to the pinnacle of success by working at Cartra, *for being chosen*. I was repeatedly reminded of this by the company and its culture. The company appeared to cater to everyone's needs in these ways, but this was mostly so that employees continued to work and didn't go home. I heard stories of employees' marriages breaking up because of the work that took priority in their life. I noticed some people that worked there had pretty big egos because of this inflation in perceived status.

Our account director from Artel, Zain, walked around like he was a rock star, wearing his sunglasses inside and sporting a daily uniform of a brightly colored polo shirt with jeans. At first, I was dazzled, but slowly I realized I didn't like this attitude of entitlement one bit. One of the Cartra client managers that needed to be kept happy was Karel, from the Czech Republic. Cartra was a big melting pot in that sense: I worked with people from all over Europe who had different ways of viewing the world. Cartra's intent with this blend of people, in open collaborative office spaces, was to create "positive friction." I'm sure that was some people's experience, but in my case it was not positive, but it did teach me to work with all sorts of different people.

Whenever Karel wasn't happy, which was most of the time, it meant trouble for our team. And, look, I get it. Our new team of ten wasn't trained properly, and it was showing up in the quality of work. If I had been the client, I would have been dissatisfied too. Unfortunately for us, as members of the team, *we* received the backlash, not our managers. I was tasked with updating Cartra's internal website for Karel, something I was brand-new to and had been given absolutely zero direction on. I did what I could by meeting with him to get his objectives and then meeting with our web developer and graphic designer to get their feedback on a timeline. When I came back to Karel, he was furious and said that what I had pulled together was unacceptable.

Zain scheduled a meeting with Karel and me. First, Zain apologized, then he made me apologize. And then he yelled at me in the client's presence. "This can't happen again!"

Afterward, I was called into a meeting with Zain and my direct manager from Artel, Quinn, who was calling in by video streamed on a flat-screen TV in the meeting room. I remember her talking head screaming at me about how I needed to be better, without giving me any tangible feedback. All I heard over and over was that I had messed up, and that it was a huge problem for Karel to be angry with us. "We cannot lose Cartra as our client!" she threatened. I was stunned. I had never been treated this way at work, or by anyone, for that matter. Without realizing it at the time, I accepted the blame for the deeper issues of productivity that had been brewing on the entire team. And this was not an isolated incident: the pressure in our workplace was so intense that most conversations were emotionally charged like this. I was humiliated for these mistakes on a regular basis and started living on edge, unsure of when people's anger would spill out. My guard was up.

I didn't know at the time that life is always a reflection of your state of mind. I felt underqualified and out of my wheelhouse, having started over in a new place. Because I felt negatively about myself, I attracted people that felt negatively about me. Because I didn't know any better, I took the fall for problems that weren't even mine. I was so new in my career; I didn't know what I needed to succeed and how to communicate that to my managers. I had such low self-worth that I didn't stand up for myself. I didn't conform or fit into the seemingly idyllic Cartra world, and I was being shown that every day. I tried to console myself with the perks of working there; even though I was treated terribly, I could still work out at the on-site gym, which had a view of the London Eye, and I could still go out on the roof deck with a freshly made latte, as if that would make it all better somehow. I learned right then and there that the culture at a company wasn't about perks, like free beer, snacks, on-site amenities, or foosball tables. It went so much deeper than that.

Whenever I didn't do something right and someone would yell at me in front of everyone else, it was as if my life were sending me a message. The message was "Get out of here!" But I didn't know that yet. Looking back, it clearly wasn't healthy to be in a work environment where people would yell at me to get their point across. I was internalizing this negative feedback as evidence of my low self-worth. I thought I deserved it. And I went along with it. I played into the "we're one happy family" trope with the team. I had been good at playing pretend while growing up with my own nuclear family too. Now, here in London, we were all a "family" on the surface, living in a cloyingly colorful, seemingly fun Cartra world. I even sought the approval of the director, like I did from my dad, and his temper was just like my dad's temper too.

When any of us showed up even a few minutes after nine o'clock, we'd get an instant message from Zain.

"You're late. Get here on time."

That's how most days usually started, as if it were the military. Once, when walking to a meeting with Quinn, as she jogged down the stairs, she turned around and instructed me, "You should *run* there with me—this is what 'agency life' is like."

I remember thinking, *This is not how I want to be living my life*—rushing around like a chicken with my head cut off. Stressing out about deadlines and making people unhappy. This felt like I was going backward in my career, even though I was in a senior role. It felt like I was an intern again—in fact, I'd been treated better as an intern. This company was not where I was supposed to be. I'd *thought* the decision I had made to come here was clear, that this *had* to be what I wanted. But I was a full-blown perfectionist, and I now saw I had just made a colossal mistake. I had never taken such a large leap in my life, and this was not the reward I had been seeking. Now that I was in this nightmare, it felt as if a cloud of shame hovered over my head, and I internalized what I expected would also be my parents' disappointment in me for doing this, for not being able to stick it out at Cartra. I cared about how this would look.

I wasn't the only one struggling in the cohort of new employees. There were a few people from Italy and Spain on my team who didn't speak English very well and were having trouble and were being made fun of too. Others just fell in line, did what they were told, and put up with the poor treatment. I was definitely struggling the most.

I remember hiding on all the different floors of Cartra, away from the cold and demanding team members and clients. I would take my laptop to the top floors and try to focus on my work there. I vividly recall sitting with my laptop perched at the edge of a bar table one day as I looked down on the streets of London from above, thinking, *I should be happy here, up above everyone, sipping my freshly made cappuccino.* But I wasn't.

I started to feel as if a pattern in my family was now playing out. I was the black sheep, and now workplace issues were burdening me instead of family issues. Growing up in the family of an alcoholic, who was also suspected to be bipolar, I felt I was expected to deny my reality of what was going on. I would stand up to my dad and make it clear that I knew what was going on with his drinking and that I saw the dysfunction that was too much to ignore. But, to me, it felt like everyone else in my family denied it, as if that would make it go away, and when I brought it up, I was blamed for even talking about something so unspeakable. The more the issue was buried, the more I made it my mission to try and solve my dad's addiction and get him to change. That was never going to be possible.

And now it wasn't my job to fix these workplace problems and all the issues from our lack of training, unclear responsibilities, team mismanagement, and unrealistic expectations. Yet I made it mine. And I took the blame. This is a typical trait of the ENFP, one of the sixteen personality types outlined in the Myers-Briggs assessment. I had taken that assessment in an off-site team training in London (one of the small silver linings from this position) and had learned that I tend toward Extroverted, iNtuitive, Feeling, and Perceiving personality traits. Often, this type of person feels like the savior in a company, and they need to determine whether they are actually the person meant to help, because things will go south if they aren't. They will be made to be the villain instead, and issues of the team will be projected onto them.

I'm the most extroverted introvert, but at a time in my life when I needed to be extroverted, my low self-esteem and lack of confidence held me back. I had so much to say and loved connecting with people, but according to the assessment, I could also be introspective and have a tendency to ponder the deeper meaning and significance of life. ENFPs see their colleagues as equals, so it made sense that I wasn't happy in this hierarchical work environment. This training started to give me insight into why this experience wasn't working. This personality type also thrives in a career with creativity and variety, but the career has to be connected to their values and needs to make a positive difference in the world. If not, ENFPs like me will find it very hard to do the job.

That's where I was. I didn't have a connection to the mission or corporate values at Cartra, or this branch of Artel, and I wasn't thriving in a role that made the most of my skill set. Even though it was more creative than my job back at home, I was still in a project management and client-facing role, rather than on a creative marketing or branding career path. My ego had been bruised, because I had to be a beginner in a new environment, when I was accustomed to being perceived as the expert back home. I had many self-esteem wounds when I took coworkers' behaviors personally. Although I'd always had a tendency to be passive-aggressive, I didn't like the escalating feelings of hostility I carried inside. I also wasn't playing into the toxic work culture on my team, where people pretended to be friends but later stabbed each other in the back. I was the one that saw through the BS this environment created, and I was the only one who finally stood up to it. But I didn't get anywhere at first with my passive-aggressive rebuttals in my interactions with my managers. So I took it to HR. My last resort.

Throughout these several months of communication breakdowns and dealing with issues surrounding project completion, a perfect storm had been evolving: new job responsibilities in a new country, a company with inadequate structures in place for the effective transfer of knowledge, and unhealthy office politics. I took action by reaching out to Artel's off-site HR person, who came into the city to meet with me at a coffee shop to hear my explanation of what was happening. *Oh, and I did not hold back.* At that point in my career, I believed conversations with HR were supposed to be confidential, that they wouldn't communicate to my team what I was about to share.

"What did you experience on your team that impacted how you could do your job?" she asked. She had arrived a few minutes later than I had, and she was wearing an eclectic, colorful outfit, with a casual pashmina scarf wrapped around her. Her friendly demeanor helped me let down my guard to share what I was going through.

"I don't have any guidance from my manager," I said. "It's unclear how I'm supposed to complete projects, and there are no processes in place that are documented. This affects how well or how timely I can complete projects for the client, and the client is never satisfied. I don't feel comfortable asking my manager or the director, because they don't know themselves what my role needs (their words; they said it was because my role was new)." I watched as she vigorously scribbled down a full page of notes based on my answers.

The next day I got an instant message from Zain. He told me to come to a meeting room, and with my heart racing, I knew this wasn't a good omen. Knowing this was probably the end of my career there, I didn't go without resisting. I responded by saying I wanted to set up a meeting at a later time, hoping that maybe he just wanted to talk about the feedback. But deep down, I knew. I wanted to prolong the inevitable, but I realized I had no choice in this matter, so I went to the room at the appointed time.

The HR assistant with whom I had spoken at the coffee shop was there, along with Zain. "Things aren't working out, and we're firing you," said Zain in a flat tone.

I didn't let them see me upset, holding in my tears, and I handed them my laptop. Zain escorted me out but not just to the elevators. He rode down the elevator with me and walked me all the way to the building's exit. He gave me one last tight-lipped glare and a smirk, and I held his gaze until he turned on his heel. I started crying immediately once I was out on the street. It was my birthday that weekend, and my grandma from France was coming to visit me that night.

My mamie, or "grandma" in French, was a devout Catholic, and she was convinced that my guardian angels had coordinated this plan for us to meet that evening. She claimed it would be a timely birthday gift and that she would help pull me out of my unhappiness, because I wouldn't be able to do it myself. Being fired was the biggest gift I could have received from the universe; I just didn't know it at the time. If you don't make a move to change your life for the better, sometimes the universe will do it for you.

Thankfully, I had my mamie visiting me in London for my birthday on the weekend after I lost my job. Even though I was in pain (you can see it in my eyes), she was meant to be there to support me.

I still hung on to my London dream, despite losing my job, because I knew how it would look if I went home so soon. I searched for jobs for nearly three months after, walking every day to a dingy internet café in my neighborhood that smelled like sweat to apply for positions, because my personal laptop had died. (Another sign that the universe wanted me out of London.) I gave it my all—I worked with recruiters and connected with alumni from my university who were living in London and met them for coffee to network. One alum referred me for a job interview at her company, but I didn't get the job. My identity of being a successful professional had been shattered and snatched away. Whatever confidence I had was shaken to its core. I couldn't fathom returning to America, because I believed that I would seem like a flake if I didn't finish what I had started. That was a false belief that I had learned through societal programming.

The reality, of course, is that you *can* change your mind at any time and course correct. You are so much more than your career. It doesn't mean you're flaky or inconsistent if you change your mind. It's smart when you make a decision to leave what isn't working.

You are so much more than your career.

But that was a lesson I had yet to learn. For the time being, I looked for a new job in London, and when I wasn't job searching, I walked around the city and sipped on cans of Pimm's cocktail, right out in the open, in broad daylight, as I walked through the parks. I would drink in public, haphazardly, on my own, to console myself—I had no shame about this. *Look, how bad could this be? I have my friend, alcohol, to help.*

But, at last, the time came for me to go back home. One spring weekend a message flashed before me like a neon billboard in the night sky: *I had to get the hell out of this city.* I booked a one-way ticket, packed up what I could, left whatever didn't fit in my luggage in the dumpster, and showed up at my mom's home on short notice and with my tail between my legs. By then, I had created a story about myself that I was broken, I sucked at my job, and I didn't know how to make the right decisions for myself. I had internalized my circumstances because I'd only been focusing on the external aspects of my life. I didn't think any company would hire me back after being fired, and I thought I could never do better than Cartra. I had been at the "best" company in the world, and I had failed. Because I'd had no previous relationship with failure, I didn't know this would serve as a stepping-stone for my next adventure.

In fact, failure is needed to move forward. If you never risk anything, you don't have the opportunity to succeed either. Failing forward is the only way you'll be able to learn, whether that's a new skill or a new business. Perfectionism had held me back for so long. Until London, I didn't want to play the game of life if there was no guarantee I would succeed. I clung to safety, as most people do. Moving to London was the first substantive risk I'd taken in my life, and even though it didn't work out as planned, it taught me all about taking risks.

Failing forward is the only way you'll be able to learn, whether that's a new skill or a new business.

Had I not tried living and working in London, I may have always looked back and regretted not giving it a try. And my experience there made me appreciate where I was from. For most of my life, I had wanted to get out of the US and live abroad. I was always comparing and complaining. But once in London, I realized there was so much more that I valued in terms of quality of living—there were more important things about what you call home than clean infrastructure, modern architecture, or a vibrant nightlife. A feeling of home wasn't all about the nightclubs—yes, that had played a surprisingly big role in my choice to move to London. Because of my experience in London, I realized I am happier at home in the US, even though I had always thought there must be *something* much better than this. I had been focused on trivial things, like how lame it was that nightclubs in my hometown near Boston closed at 1:00 a.m., instead of staying open until 8:00 a.m. I hadn't realized how superficial my life really was until I moved across the ocean. It forced me to start looking deeper at what I value.

By moving to London, I also set myself up to later learn how to become comfortable with ambiguity and create my own life path, even if it looked completely different from that of everyone around me and even if it meant making some mistakes that ultimately propelled me closer to what I really wanted. London set a precedent for doing what I wanted to do, following through on my dreams, even if I was scared and unsure of what would happen. It eventually made me realize that I didn't need others to buy in to my life choices. I had to look within as I made my next move.

CHAPTER 3

New York City

As you start to walk out on the way, the way
appears.

—Rumi

In an attempt to get back to what I knew, I tried to get another
position with Artel in the Boston location, also based on advice
from my family. Before I had left the Boston office for London,
I had referred a friend for my old position, and she was thriving in it, so that role wasn't available. I thought I'd sealed off
the doorway to my previous life, until I connected with a former colleague based in Texas who, even though he wasn't with
Artel anymore, connected me with his manager in Artel's New
York office.

I went into this conversation with the low self-esteem I was
carrying from my London experience. It was difficult to trust
myself now. It was difficult to trust this company again, too,
even though my experience in the Boston office was nothing
like what I'd experienced with Cartra in London. Yet I was

desperate to get back on track, to my old life where I had been climbing up the ladder successfully, even if not happily. It was my safety net.

A role was open in New York, so I went down for the day for a five-hour interview. I figured New York City was like London, but it would be closer to home and in the same country this time. This could be my second shot. I was thrilled that I got the job and that my previous departure hadn't held me back. The next step was to secure housing. I connected with one of my mom's friends, who had just learned that her friend's daughter was looking for a roommate in the Murray Hill area. And just like that I was off again, less than three months after I had come home from London. This move went a lot smoother than London had right off the bat, considering I already had a place to live before arriving.

New York City energy, however, was another sensory overload. I realized that, compared to living in London, which was a little quieter, I was able to feel these loud city-life sensations on a deep level. Every car horn startled me, and the constant vibration of construction drills could be felt through every cell of my body. One afternoon, after feeling wiped out from simply walking down the sidewalk, I went online and started looking up "feeling tired from noise and lights." Was this a real thing? In my Googling, I found the term "highly sensitive person," coined by psychologist Elaine Aron. Those with high levels of sensitivity, roughly 15–20 percent of the population, display increased emotional sensitivity and stronger reactivity to both external and internal stimuli—pain, hunger, light, and noise. Once I read the description, I realized I must be a highly sensitive person, as my mind was never truly still in this environment. I always felt on high alert, unable to relax, and my nervous system buzzed right along with the city. This feeling of being constantly stimulated made it difficult for me to even think straight. Having a framework to understand what I was experiencing was helpful, and it started my growth toward understanding and accepting myself.

Despite the sensory overload, it felt fresh and exciting to launch a new adventure by moving to New York. Once again, I could start over where no one knew who I was, and I could put the past behind me. I did not speak about London to anyone at all. That was the past. I was going to prove to everyone, this time, that I could do this. The move was so easy compared to my London relocation, most likely due to the fact that I had already done it on a much larger scale.

In fact, moving to London had opened me to a whole new power and possibility for what I could achieve with my life. A bold move like that can change a person, and in a way, it grounded me into being more of who I am. I was no longer the small-town girl bumbling around the big, foreign city. I had been yearning to get out of the bubble and create a new story for myself, apart from those limiting stories that had been crafted by the people whom I had lived with, and known, my whole life.

The transfer to London had accomplished that goal, and now I was able to approach my New York enterprise with more confidence than I'd had before. New York would be a different type of medicine for me. This was going to be my second chance. But I hadn't healed from the experience in London. I still carried that emotional baggage with me, locked in a closet within, and was hoping this new exploit would redeem me. Life keeps bringing back similar events in an attempt to heal us because, when making a different choice in a similar situation, there is an opportunity to transmute the old wound. New York would be my opportunity to heal from London.

So there I was on one sunny day, the first weekend in June, arriving in New York City and dazzled by the unending activities and places I could explore: rooftop bars, free pop-up concerts, the ferry to Governors Island, and even the beach along

New Jersey. I had never had this many options—not even in London—and the warm weather made this an open and inviting season to begin my new adventure. A much better welcome than my prior move.

On my first day at work, there were a lot of people my age to bond with. Coming from a place where I had had no friends, I welcomed this reprieve. I already knew a colleague from my team in Boston, back before I'd moved to London, who had since transferred to the New York office. I joined the office book club that met in the beer garden by the East River after work. I played tour guide for friends and family who visited, and I also spent time with my roommates, with whom I shared a modern apartment that was exquisitely decorated and had doormen, a laundry service, and a private balcony overlooking the East River.

The people I met in New York were unique and bold. Some were in the music industry, some were nurses, some were wellness entrepreneurs, and some were in my own industry— marketing. Yet their occupations weren't what necessarily defined them. They were creative, with many interests, and they were go-getters. They were independent even though they were connected. This was new for me, seeing people confident enough to stand on their own, have multidimensional lives, and exhibit passion about their work.

Photobooth fun with my friends and colleagues in New York City at a House of Vans concert in Brooklyn. One of the things I loved about New York was that I never ran out of fun experiences.

This discovery, and being exposed to their energy, marked the beginning of developing these aspects of myself and being able to become my own person. Not the person my parents wanted me to be. Or the person that society wanted me to be. From those perspectives, I felt I was supposed to be a good girl who colored inside the lines, grew her career, got married, bought a house, and had kids. I wasn't initially aware that a different script might be available for me. The real me, I was learning, was multifaceted. I could get angry and sad as much as I could have fun, be creative, and enjoy new experiences. I

was a bit of a rebel. I wanted the opposite of the plan that society had laid out for me. I wanted to live an unconventional life,
but I'd been too afraid to step off the track I was on.

My friends here were so individual and so free, and they
taught me to be the same. I would not be put in a box anymore. It felt to me as though people in New York City were
much more open and friendly than they had been in London,
where I'd struggled to break into established friend circles. It
took only a few months to get really close with my new group
of friends in New York, and I remember feeling relieved once
I did. The ease with which all this happened had to do with
my own view of New York, along with my renewed sense of
adventure.

Yet it was also easy to be alone for a bit in the city—easier
than it had been for me in London. I went to free events that
interested me on my own. I checked out museums and saw the
sights, never running out of things to do. Whether it was a day
trip to Governors Island or an evening out at a free stand-up
comedy show at a Lower East Side bar, I had fun exploring by
myself. I enjoyed my own company for the first time. Unlike in
London, I didn't feel the heavy pang of loneliness in my being.
I had learned how to be more on my own there, and now New
York felt inviting to me in spite of that fact that I arrived alone.

Just like in London, however, the honeymoon period dis-
sipated as I started to settle in. Once again, I was not in a role
at work that was playing on my strengths, and because of that
I was not on a team that I worked well with. *Shit.* That sink-
ing feeling came back, as I realized I was in the wrong career,
again. It didn't help that I carried the last story of my work
with me and was constantly on guard. Still not fully healed,
I again began to approach challenges from the victim standpoint. Yet I had to make this work.

I'd been harassed as an adult in the London office, where
irate supervisors had talked down to me and gossiping

colleagues had stabbed me in the back. It was worse than high school bullying, much worse. But in some respects, being a victim made things easy because I didn't have to take responsibility and could blame problems on someone or something else. I could also rely on external factors to assess my self-worth. What type of job I had, the clothes and makeup I wore, the relationships I had, and the social activities I'd entered on my calendar all factored into my view of myself, along with how I believed other people perceived me.

My self-worth was especially affected by external factors in my job. Being accepted as a successful person at the company, and in society overall, made me feel as if I was important, a feeling I continued to crave because I wasn't able to validate myself. I went to client dinners in upscale restaurants, attended company outings on booze cruises, and traveled to our major hotel client in Maryland for meetings. This was still the life I thought I wanted, the life I'd chased in London, and I felt like I'd *made it*. But it was just a continuation of the London angst. My identity was still my corporate self.

Underneath the shiny exterior, though, I was going through the motions. Something was off. I wasn't engaged or energized by my work. I counted down the hours until it was time to go home, shopped online to numb myself, and tried my best to avoid conflicts with colleagues. Early in this role I was introduced to the term "CYA," meaning "cover your ass." That was all that mattered: as long as you could show your face to your team and especially the client, no matter who you threw under the bus, you would be okay. At least that's how I took it. I found myself complaining to friends that I was in the wrong role and that one of the managers on my team was horrible to me. My friends would all agree. By just complaining, though, I was not taking responsibility or changing anything. In one way, I loved that victim story because it gave me an excuse for not making the drastic and difficult changes that I needed to make. I could just complain about it. But it kept me stuck.

Outside work, I relied on my mom and sister for emotional support. My sister, Lara, helped me move to New York and stayed with me that first weekend. My mom would also visit, and we would enjoy going to the Halloween parade, volunteering at the New York City marathon, and running a French 5K in Central Park together. My relationship with my dad was on hold, by choice. I had cut off contact with him when I was studying abroad in Florence because of the effect his alcohol use had on me. The last meaningful conversation I remember having with him was an hour on the phone there. I stood in the lobby of my apartment homestay, not caring that it was an expensive international call on my cell. He and I were talking in a more open way now that I was halfway around the world.

That was the last time I felt connected to him. Soon after that call, once I had returned home to Boston, I had to enforce no contact. I did this because, most of the time, my dad's words made no sense when he reached out to me. His emails were troubling and gave me a clue that his sanity was slipping away from him. Sometimes I would get late-night drunken texts from him, begging me to tell him I loved him.

"Hi Dad," I wrote back. "I won't be responding to your emails or calls. I need to take a break. It's hurting too much. I love you."

This was the last email I sent, and then I blocked his phone number. He didn't listen, at first, and he kept sending emails. Eventually, when I didn't respond, he stopped. I continued to worry a great deal about how he wasn't getting better. His health and our relationship were always in the back of my mind, and our estrangement had an effect on my mental health. I felt abandoned, betrayed. I felt unlovable because, no matter how much I tried, my dad would not change, he could not be there for me the way I needed him to be. So I filled my life with distractions. I put enormous pressure on myself to achieve and perform, almost as if my success would make him see the light and he'd just stop drinking for me, for all of us in our family. My dad would get better because of my achievements. Surely, he wouldn't want to miss out on that? Of course, at the time, I didn't realize I was doing this to cope with the pain, as I kept trying to make things better at work.

There was a silver lining to this role, though, just like there had been in London. A VP on my team, who sat next to me in an office with walls of glass, was someone I respected and learned a great deal from, even from watching him interact with others and lead. Matthew was an example I could look up to. He was someone who actively looked for the best in people, and when I went to him seeking guidance on my struggles, he said, "Seek first to understand, then to be understood." This was what I needed to hear in order to get myself out of victim mode regarding these disagreements on my team, and it's a reminder I still come back to today. Then he left the company.

Things at work weren't improving. I started to realize that I was going to have to either put up with the way things were or quit. I interviewed for other jobs but wasn't getting many leads. So, I decided I'd have to accept my circumstances as they were. I don't blame myself for doing this: Isn't that why so many people stay in jobs they're miserable in? They think they don't have an option, and sometimes they don't. Most of the time, however, they do. It's fear of the unknown that usually keeps people stuck—fear that they won't have money or they won't land successfully on their feet somewhere else. Better the devil you know than the one you don't.

Anyone who's been in a similar situation knows that when you don't get along with colleagues and the company culture doesn't facilitate resolution, it becomes unbearable having to spend so much of your life at work. Its effects on your psyche ripple out into every area of your life. In this role, I learned a lot about the importance of company culture, as a continuation of the lessons I'd learned in London, and the well-being it provides for employees, if fostered intentionally. When I had downtime, I went for long walks along the pier in the Financial District, to a row of Adirondack chairs on an elevated deck, where I sat in the sun and listened to music, as my little escape. I was drinking around five to six cups of coffee a day just to feel alive and meet my baseline—a sign that what I was doing with my life wasn't giving me energy, it was depleting me. I had learned to become numb, ignoring everything that my soul screamed for me to change. I still held on, because I didn't feel I had the option to leave. I believed I had what most people dreamed of—a successful job and an overall privileged life— and I didn't want to go through failure again. An immigrant mindset of clinging to security was still with me.

And then along came another depressing, disillusioning day on March 15, 2016, when my soul was completely checked out, as usual. It was raining, so, unable to make it to my Adirondack chair to escape, I sat in the open-plan cubicle (my personal hell, as I was an introvert, albeit a more extroverted one), with no windows to see outside. I was surrounded by coworkers whom I felt at war with, staring blankly at my Outlook, unsure what to work on, but also constantly on guard, with my fight-or-flight instincts activated by the energy of the city and the stress-laden office. And then a call came in on my cell phone that would change my life's trajectory.

CHAPTER 4

The Phone Call

Grief can be the garden of compassion. If you
keep your heart open through everything,
your pain can become your greatest ally in
your life's search for love and wisdom.

—Rumi

I saw that the call's area code was from the town where I had
grown up. I hadn't heard anything from there for so long. It
had been years since my mom and sister had moved away, and
only my dad remained there. My mind immediately flashed
back to my childhood home, set high up off the street on a
hill, surrounded by evergreen shrubs and a few oak trees. It
was a small town of around twenty thousand people, where
my younger days were spent walking around the neighborhood with friends. Fond memories of summers spent outdoors, swimming at my neighbor's pool, and winters spent
sledding down the hill in front of my house flooded my senses.

I normally didn't answer calls from random numbers, but I instantly knew this one wasn't normal.

I picked up, and the person on the other line introduced himself as a police officer.

"Miss Smith? This is Officer Houston from the Stoneham Police Department. I'm afraid I'm calling with some bad news."

I knew his name; he had taught in the D.A.R.E. (Drug Abuse Resistance Education) program in my school throughout my childhood.

The moment he said his name, I knew what had happened. I started to cry uncontrollably. Tears welled, blurring my vision. My breath caught, and my stomach dropped. A terrible choking feeling spread throughout my chest. It had been a while since I'd heard from my dad; he was in his "dormant" phase, as the rest of my family called it. In his angry and agitated phase, he would contact us nonstop via every possible means. But then he would go dormant for months, and we wouldn't hear anything from him. We suspected these patterns were related to undiagnosed bipolar disorder, which he likely self-medicated with alcohol. When you love an alcoholic, you dread the day that you receive the call that something terrible has finally happened. The police were calling me because I was next of kin, the next in line for the inheritance, as the oldest child.

"We found your dad, who passed away at his house," Officer Houston said.

"What happened?" I asked, even though I knew the answer.

"Well, we found him surrounded by empty bottles of alcohol," he said, with a flat and slightly judgmental tone. "It's not clear when your dad died. One of his friends noticed he hadn't heard from your dad on Facebook for about a week, and so he called us."

My dad had an online presence that my family and I didn't know much about; he spent a lot of time on forums, internet games, and Facebook, so this was a friend he had met online. I didn't feel sympathy from the officer; he just gave me the facts. This call was just another routine task he was checking off his list for the day. It was probably not the first time he had experienced this. Still, I was furious, as well as sad. So many emotions were hitting me at once that I could hardly speak.

I found a conference room so that I could cry, even though the walls were all glass. Thankfully, no one was around at that moment. And then, when I felt the heaviness and tension in my body melt away with the tears, I knew something had changed inside me. I had finally let go of all the dark emotions buried so deep within me, which I didn't know were there. I had never given myself space to feel these emotions, and it was a relief to finally feel *something*, even if it was the most intense type of excruciating sadness. Without knowing why, it was clear to me that, in that moment, my life had just changed completely, as if I had been unknowingly holding my breath for years and years and it now came rushing out like a gust of wind.

Before this phone call, I had been completely disconnected from my emotions. Without even realizing it, I had bottled up every emotion over the years. I pretended nothing wrong was happening until something finally set me off. I would only typically cry hysterically for reasons that didn't even have anything to do with the issue at hand. Invariably, these crying jags would happen only when I'd been drinking.

Somehow, I went back to work for the rest of the day. Yet again, I wanted to pretend that nothing was wrong and that I was strong. And it made sense that I'd do this, even in light of this family news, because I was known as the "strong" one in my family, which just meant I held on to everybody's emotions for them, like an emotional dumping ground.

I think I was viewed in this way because I had survived leukemia when I was three. I hadn't allowed myself to feel the sadness of that period in my life. In the following years, when my dad would have a drunken blowup and get in a car crash or get in a fight at a family friend's get-together, I'd be upset and my mom would say, "You're the strong one in the family—you can get through this." I knew this was a well-meant sentiment, but at the time, it didn't allow me to feel my own emotions. I was the strong one who held my family together, because that made it easier for everyone, rather than having to deal with the raw emotions of imperfect human beings. I interpreted being strong to mean being emotionless.

Later that week, I cried as I left the office for the day, and as I walked down the street on the way to a dentist appointment, in the faintly misting rain, no one batted an eye. It was a moment when I felt grateful for being invisible in New York City, so I could continue to release the years of pain in peace.

On this walk, I spoke on the phone with my godfather, Bruce, my dad's best friend. When I stopped at the corner of Liberty Street and Broadway, outside the dentist's office, amid the five o'clock commuters bustling by, Bruce said the kindest things to me I felt I had ever heard, and he promised to be there for me as a father figure for the rest of my life. Our bond grew stronger from that day, and it was as if I could feel my dad's love for me through him.

"When you need me, call on me; like a warm blanket you can grab the corner of, I will always be there to love, support, and keep you warm," he said through choked-back tears. "Your dad was my best friend. He loved you very much, and he wanted me to be there for you when he was gone."

Me with my dad on vacation at Walt Disney World Resort. A reminder of the fun we had together amid the pain.

My dad's passing was the start of me feeling the true nature of his love, which I had never been able to experience previously. It sounds strange, but I had heard that he loved me from his friends and my family more than I had ever heard it from him. He had expressed his love in a different way from how I would have liked to feel it.

Me and my dear godfather, Bruce, reunited at my sister's wedding in France in 2019.
He has played a huge role in my life. Knowing I have his support and love has helped
me heal and move forward after my dad's passing.

Grief cracked me open in the way I needed it to. My heart
had been closed up; I had put up walls because of the many
challenges that had disrupted my life. After breaking up with
my high school sweetheart of four years before I left for university, I closed my heart off to love. I closed my heart a little
more when my parents got divorced while I was in university. I
didn't love the work I did for my career, and I closed myself off
from the possibility of passion.

I didn't know who I was anymore because I had created my
life based on what I saw around me and on how my parents had
lived. I wasn't living my own life. My dad's death put life into
perspective and showed me how I had been pretending that he
wouldn't die one day. I even had so much resistance to going
to his memorial, like I was denying that this was the reality.
I'm glad I went, as it ended up being such a sweet experience,

where I talked with people who had known and loved him. We celebrated his life, instead of mourning it.

Suddenly, I realized time wasn't infinite, as much as Western society pretends it is. This revelation lit a fire in me, so to speak, as if I was given a new lease on life. Once I realized this, I ever so slowly started making changes to make my life count.

CHAPTER 5

Alcoholism

Knowing your own darkness is the best
method for dealing with the darknesses of
other people.

—Carl Jung

My dad's passing from alcoholism was something I knew
might happen; it was just a matter of time. No one can ever
prepare for something like this, and it seemed to happen when
I needed to wake up from the trance of the inauthentic life I
was living. Death can do that.

Alcohol had been a part of my family's life for as long as
I could remember. Gatherings at our home always featured
wine and beer, sometimes cocktails. Children can pick up on
everything, and ever since I was young, I knew that alcohol
was what my family used to blow off steam. But when used in
excess, alcohol made my home feel volatile, unsafe. As a child
growing up, I looked to my parents as a source of safety and
emotional regulation. When I couldn't count on that, I slowly

started to lose trust and the ability to feel physically safe. Even while not drinking, my dad was an abrasive and unpredictable person. One day he would be chatting up a stranger at the grocery store in friendly conversation, and the next he would be yelling at my friends who were waiting for me outside the house, on bikes, to leave. Or he would fly off the handle over something I would say and scream at me with vitriol. He often said, "Children should be seen, not heard," which is likely what he had heard growing up too. I never knew what version of my dad I would get, and alcohol in the mix only amplified these behaviors. I just wanted a dad that would love and support me—and maybe not embarrass me by being so *grouchy* all the time.

Someone who's hard to love can sometimes be better understood through their own upbringing. My father grew up in Arbroath, Scotland, a quaint fishing town on the North Sea coast of the country. Drinking is a typical pastime there, as it is in the country as a whole. Although I loved visiting each year while growing up, I always sensed an overwhelming feeling of sadness in the air of his perpetually gray and rainy hometown that was numbed by afternoons at the pub or with nightcaps. My father started drinking at the age of twelve, and his parents allowed him to do this. At that time, it was the norm for kids to drink alongside their parents in Scotland. According to the Substance Abuse and Mental Health Services Administration's National Survey on Drug Use and Health in the US, youth alcohol use is a solid predictor of substance use disorders in later life. I started drinking at age fourteen, so I wasn't too far off either.

With my dad on what I believe was my ninth birthday. Even during a celebratory time, there were signs that he wasn't well—his empty drink was close by.

No one turns into an alcoholic or addict on purpose. In Europe, where my parents were raised, children are served alcohol at a young age. As my dad's life stressors became too much for him, this pattern allowed alcohol to become the trusted solution. Until it wasn't. My mom is from France, where there is a similar drinking culture, except with mostly wine instead of whiskey. She wasn't alcoholic, and it seemed she played more of an enabling role for my dad's addiction, even though she did take steps to introduce him to therapy and AA. She stuck it out for him, hoping he'd get better, and when he wasn't emotionally available, she leaned on me to provide that support for her. Don't get me wrong, I love my family deeply. I believe you get the family you're born into for a reason—to grow. But I had to come to terms with how I was influenced by their behaviors and patterns.

While my mom, Christine, was able to provide me with safety from my dad, it wasn't until I was an adult that I realized the imbalance in my relationship with her, where I couldn't feel all my feelings. I knew how much she sacrificed for me, and I knew how difficult it was living with my dad. I depended a lot on my mom, too, and in this dynamic I unconsciously strived to meet *her* emotional needs so that *I* could feel safe. I was put in this role, as each member plays a different role in families, in a way that helps them "survive" or get their needs met. I also extended this role to Lara. I felt emotionally responsible for her as a result of my relationship with my mom, albeit without Lara intending this. I was the older sister, so I had to look out for Lara and meet her needs. It gave me an ego boost, no doubt, to be looked up to in this way.

There were times at dinner when it was clear my dad was inebriated, but we just didn't address it. In classic fashion for a family with an alcoholic, the not-so-secret issue was ignored. With this, I learned it wasn't safe to trust myself, because my perception of reality was denied.

"You're drunk," I would say to my dad.

"Nope. No, I'm not," my dad would exclaim, shaking his head vigorously from side to side. That was what typically happened: he would never admit it. Yet I was sure of it. *Or was I?*

Water bottles filled with hard alcohol started turning up behind couch pillows when I was fifteen. Because of this concrete evidence, my mom insisted we all start seeing a therapist, the same therapist my dad would see on his own after my mom asked him to. Alcoholism rarely just affects the person with the addiction; it has a ripple effect on all the other people in their life. Later, in my twenties, I had a friend whose dad was also an addict and an alcoholic, but he had been able to get sober. Even then, she had felt the effects of it on her psyche while growing up. Just a few years after I graduated university, she invited me to an Al-Anon group, which is part of AA but for members of the affected family. At this group's meeting, I realized she had alcoholic tendencies, too, just like me—ironically, we would split scorpion bowl cocktails before going.

Once, when Lara and I went to a therapy session with my dad to confront him about drinking, he didn't look in our eyes for the entire hour. He stared blankly at the wall instead. Almost as if we weren't there. When my dad's alcoholism came to a head, my mom made the incredibly brave decision to divorce him. She drew a line in the sand for what she would tolerate, and she never looked back. She'd held out as long as she could for the sake of my sister and me. I don't believe it was any specific event that tipped the scales; it was more the fact that she had tried every possible way to help, and the disease was getting worse.

This taught me an important lesson that I wouldn't fully realize until I experienced it personally in one of my romantic relationships—that love is not enough to save someone. They have to want to be saved. It is toxic to try and save someone from themselves. You can never do someone else's inner work for them, and the only way people change is when they decide to, especially when it comes to addiction.

Love is not enough to save someone.

Deep down, I believe that any person suffering from alcoholism or addiction wants to be saved, but sometimes the need to extinguish their pain in the moment is louder than their desire to heal. Alcoholism can be looked at through many different lenses. There's the physical dependence, where your body craves alcohol and you can even die when you stop drinking cold turkey. There's the emotional lens, where alcohol becomes a tool to manage and numb emotions. Then there's a spiritual lens, and this is where I'm fascinated. To me, alcohol can be a tool that invites negative entities to possess someone's body and soul. Why is alcohol called "spirits," after all? Being with someone that's under the influence often gives me the impression that they are truly not there. And when someone is blacked out, there's sometimes a vacant look in their eyes as they go about their lives, having full conversations with people, walking around, and making decisions that they won't even remember the next day. Alcohol is like a puppet master, dragging their bodies to and fro. Sometimes an alter ego even takes over, making the person scream or dance or otherwise behave in a way they normally wouldn't.

In my own experience, I would become a different person, and my true self would shut down when I was under the influence. In my sorority, I was voted "closet party girl" because, in daily life, I was introverted, sweet, and polished. People who partied with me would be so surprised to find out how I was when I wasn't drinking because, when I drank, I became outgoing, rebellious, and definitely *not* polished.

If someone doesn't have the tools or support, they can fall under this negative spiritual influence. It doesn't matter if you're smart, successful, or powerful: my dad was all those things. He was a vice president of marketing for several global corporations throughout his career, traveling all over the world for his work, even as far as Australia and Israel. Though he was not perfect and had many demons, including a suspected underlying mental illness, being an alcoholic was not his true self. That label unjustly personifies the disease, as if it were the actual person inside.

I learned how damaging that label was after my dad passed. I spent much of my life angry at the disease and, as a result, at him. My heart had closed long ago when I realized I wasn't going to get the dad I thought I needed—the dad I deserved. I saw things in black and white back then.

It took his passing for me to realize that he had another side to him that did love me, even if it wasn't in the way I wanted. He was overprotective, for example, yelling at any boys who stopped by my house, even though they were friends of mine. Although he was doing this to keep me safe, I heard a subconscious message that men were to be feared. But at the same time, he went all out on my birthdays, baking elaborate cakes that went along with the party themes, like a science party with a computer cake and a basketball party with a basketball-shaped cake. I wished he had had the capacity to show up for me the rest of the year, but he was either traveling for work or jet-lagged from his travels.

He was also his own person, apart from being a dad. We had a lot in common, which is one reason why we might have butted heads so often. My dad had many passions, including a love for cooking. He was a complete foodie and a talented chef. Our living room bookcase spanned the length of the wall and had two full rows of cookbooks: the top row was his, and as I caught the cooking bug from him, I got the second row. My dad especially loved to grill, all year round, and his cooking incorporated different cultures, such as French, Asian, and Indian. I loved going to the grocery store with him on Saturdays, helping him get all the ingredients for the upcoming week and making sure I could cook some meals too.

He got certified in scuba diving, which I developed a passion for while on vacation in the Canary Islands, when I lived in London. He also enjoyed finding eccentric, cool things to do. For example, when the internet first started (hard to imagine), he figured out he could make money by purchasing domain URLs and selling them back to people at a higher rate. And he became a lord through a process that simply involved purchasing a two-foot-square plot of land in Scotland. He was always doing funny things like that, and he had plenty of dad jokes to share, which typically made me laugh 5 percent of the time and made my eyes roll to the back of my head the rest of the time. He had a secret creative side: he wrote and sold a screenplay, which I didn't really know anything about other than that he was proud of his creation. And knowing that someday he would die, he'd had his will drawn up a few years before he passed, which showed that he cared about our family. He was smart about his money and knowledgeable with investing, and he loved to spend as much as he loved to save. I am now grateful he finished the will when he did, even if at the time I felt scared, because it let me know that his death was inevitable. Alcoholism can be like a slow and unintentional suicide.

My dad's refusal to get sober didn't mean he didn't love me. People's souls choose different paths, and I believe my dad's soul chose to be addicted as his karma. Everything does happen for a reason, and one of the (many) ultimate gifts he gave me was freedom from the power alcohol had over me. Alcohol became *much* less pleasurable after he died, and my therapist told me that I could think of this as a gift from my dad—a gift to break this legacy of addiction and choose a different path of healing.

People have both good and bad traits. No one is all good or all bad, even if it looks like it on the outside. That's one of the most important lessons I learned from my dad, and my family in general. We went on desirable family vacations, like a California road trip and a tropical getaway to the Cayman Islands. We also had financial hardships when my dad would get laid off, and living with uncertainty created a lot of emotional turbulence. On my twenty-first birthday, I wanted both my mom and dad there to celebrate, even though they had divorced while I was abroad in Italy. My dad told my mom he wanted to come, and I thought he could handle it. At brunch that morning in Harvard Square, he showed up and started to read from a letter he had written, apologizing to me and the rest of my family and asking to be part of the family again.

Except, halfway through reading it, he lost consciousness. All of a sudden, my dad's head slumped, his speech cut short, and even as I reached over to shake him and my mom repeated his name over and over, he wouldn't wake.

We were about to call 911—because he wasn't moving, despite our efforts to rouse him—when he suddenly came to. Tears streamed down my face, partly because of the sadness in seeing my dad this way and partly due to the shame and embarrassment I felt in this nice restaurant with our dark family secret out in the open. My tears continued to fall as my family assisted my dad to the garage, where he had parked. My younger sister was tasked with driving him home in his car, as we weren't sure of the reason for his fainting spell. Later that night, my mom took me to a fancy hotel in Boston for dinner and drinks with my sister as part of my birthday plans. In all the photos, my eyes are puffy and my face blotchy from crying over the shock of my dad's behavior and the disappointment in how he'd ruined my day. I was consoled with a cosmopolitan that I could sip legally for the first time. I learned this was how I could comfort myself.

My parents had their patterns from childhood that they brought into their parenting and that weren't the most functional or supportive. We had some of the highest highs and the lowest lows, and when my father passed away, that was all I knew. But as the years have progressed, I've come to learn to appreciate everything my parents did for me and to also be honest with myself about what still needs healing in me, even after all this time.

Most people live their lives on a pendulum, swinging from pain to pleasure and back again, if they're not conscious of their minds and emotions. As I grew up, this pendulum showed up in my family as periods of joy, success, and financial abundance followed by periods of strife, pain, and financial deficit. This pattern is even more true for someone living with mental illness or under the influence of addiction. Once I stopped drinking, I learned that I didn't need to be controlled by the pendulum. There is such a thing as peaceful excitement from day to day, which I began to access by being mindful of my emotions and mindset and shifting toward a more balanced and neutral state when needed. I started being drawn to peaceful experiences instead of ones that created drama.

After my dad's death, I craved the familiarity that living close to home brings. Once I was back in Boston, and removed from the challenging and unhealthy environment in New York, I had the space to process what I had gone through, and I began to learn how to acquire the tools necessary to navigate my path forward.

CHAPTER 6

Toxic Cocktail

Wholeness is not achieved by cutting off a
portion of one's being, but by integration of
the contraries.

—Carl Jung

I was heading into uncharted territory. It was now August
2016, and it had been five months since my dad passed away.
Looking back, it's no wonder I got addicted to alcohol. It had
surrounded me in unhealthy ways from a young age at home
and on the TV shows I watched, where underage drinking was
glamorized along with blacking out and getting into all sorts
of other trouble. I was so impressionable, and I copied exactly
what was being shown to me. Self-destruction was the hip
thing to do. Idolized, even. That's not by accident either; alcohol is society's favorite drug. It's widely available and serves as
a social-gathering centerpiece. It's the easiest way to numb the
pain and lubricate discomfort.

I'd always known I was different from most of my peers when I was growing up, and that uncomfortable feeling continued into adulthood. I was a deeply creative and highly sensitive child, without fully nurturing this aspect of myself. I had intense emotions I couldn't always channel in productive ways. I was foreign, having been born in Scotland, so I had a different worldview from the people at school. I didn't feel completely part of the small-town bubble. Growing up in a suburban town in the US, I became acutely aware of how I, as a first-generation kid, was different. With my family, we ate different foods, celebrated different holidays, spoke different languages, and visited family in Europe. I didn't always understand cultural norms and was embarrassed when I didn't in front of others.

Frequent hospital visits for treating leukemia while I was in preschool, at such a developmental age, also made me feel separate from my peers then and later in my life. It didn't help when I lost all my hair from the chemotherapy and kids would ask me if I was a boy or a girl. I was the "cancer kid." At a time when other children were playing and learning, I was getting blood transfusions, bone marrow transplants, and radiation. I was going through these intense procedures, growing up quickly in the process, and I was aware, even at that age, that I wasn't the same as my peers.

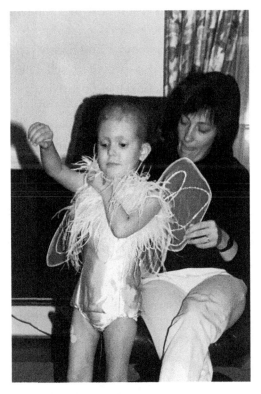

My mom helping me with my fairy costume. If it had been up to me, I would have worn costumes every day while growing up; it was one of the ways I could feel good about myself—through fantasy.

I felt I was rarely in an environment where I could be myself. At home, we didn't talk about emotions, and I felt like I blended into the family identity rather than having my own. I tried my hardest to fit into my surroundings and become just like my peers. That constant undercurrent of anxiety from treatments stayed with me from childhood on, and, combined with the stressors of living with a parent addicted to alcohol, somehow alcohol seemed the easiest soothing support. It was what I knew.

So I drank, initially, with my high school friends to drive away all those inhibitions I had while sober. At first, as usually happens with addiction, my use of alcohol wasn't a big deal. I was having fun just by the mere act of drinking. It felt rebellious. Drinking was the way to fit in and let loose. I didn't see how dangerous it was because we're not shown that side of alcohol through society's marketing. In middle school, we had the D.A.R.E. program, which leaned heavily toward promoting complete abstinence from drugs and alcohol, rather than tips for safe use. I took it seriously at the time. But when all my peers started drinking, that learning became a distant memory. Comical, even.

Knowing that my dad had an issue with alcohol just made me more susceptible to going overboard. My therapist later told me I was genetically predisposed, and I learned about drinking from watching my dad. It was inevitable. I also went to a high school where heavy drinking was the norm, although that should not have been an excuse. Kids were getting their stomachs pumped after drinking at school events, and even then, all the possible complications that could arise from alcohol abuse still seemed too far away to affect me. *That was them*, not me. Drinking was also a way to pass the time.

At first, I didn't drink too often—maybe a couple of times a month at most—but when I did, it was a night of hard drinking with vodka, endless beers, or tequila. This was how my habit of drinking in excess began. Since the opportunities were few and far between, I made the most of them. This habit carried on throughout university and only grew more dangerous over time.

As an adult, I now recognize there were many disturbing scenarios I saw on TV that were normalized for me at the age of fourteen: girls were sexually assaulted by their male "friends" while under the influence of alcohol (hello, first episode of *Gossip Girl*), and then the girls continued to be friends with them afterward, or they were dropped off by their friends outside their home, drunk and blacked out, left at the front door (as shown in *The O.C.*—which, unsurprisingly, would later happen to me too).

It was uncanny how some of these scenarios played out in my life; one might say that's just what teenagers do, but I wonder how different it would have been for me if the popular shows at that time had been a more positive influence, showing young people being creative, following their passions, and making a difference in the world—instead of giving influential programming for the exact opposite—when young people's brains are still developing.

What we watch on TV and in movies makes an impression on us and influences our behaviors, both positively and negatively, in the same way that our home lives and social lives do. And the forbidden aspect of drinking made me want it even more. Tied together with the insecurities I felt and the pain I experienced in my own home, the glamorization of alcohol served as the perfect setup for my own addiction to be born. I had a low sense of self-worth, from not feeling seen at home, and based my worth on being "chosen" by my friends, or by boys. I also placed a lot of stock in how I looked. I spent hours straightening my hair to oblivion, applying way too much self-tanner, and shopping for outfits at the mall to look my best.

My thirst for alcohol only grew, and I had the freedom to experience it without repercussions at university. But the truth was that I had used it for so long by then that I had developed a pattern of seeking an outside substance to quell the discomfort of being myself. I'd also used it to feel cool.

My time in the grip of drugs and alcohol continued while I studied abroad in Italy. I had learned about MDMA (a psychoactive substance) in 2011, before leaving for Europe; one of my male friends showed me and my roommate a study from Harvard reporting that MDMA was safe and even beneficial for mood. *If this drug had Harvard's seal of approval, maybe it wasn't so bad,* I told myself. This same friend brought ecstasy, a diluted version of pure MDMA, on a trip to Montreal for a concert, but I wasn't ready to dabble in it at that point. Later that year, during my time in Europe in the fall, I had an opportunity to try pure MDMA. This time, I was well aware of how it worked and prepared to try it.

On a weekend trip to Prague, I did MDMA for the first time at a concert with a friend who was studying abroad there, and I fell in love with the effects I experienced. I took the drug while drinking, which was not recommended, and it gave me the energy to stay awake until the sun came up at seven o'clock. Throughout the long night, I felt the music from the performance move through my body and my heart. Every note sparked a chill or evoked a new emotion of connectedness and freedom. Because the drug opened our hearts and heightened our sensory experiences, it made us feel connected and joyful, and we had no trouble hugging and holding on to each other. Intimacy was amplified. Colors and lights were also more vivid under this influence, and the lighting for the performance hypnotized and delighted us. I felt invincible, full of love and peace, and so connected and supported by the group I was with. A group of strangers from all over the US, in this foreign city, turned into friends for that night only. Later, I liked that I could remember most of the evening, which wasn't possible for me when drinking alcohol. Instead of being a depressant like alcohol, MDMA was a stimulant, and I reveled in that feeling of ease, of peace and joy, that I had been missing for so long.

But what goes up must come down, and the comedown from this drug was akin to a major depressive episode, after the levels of serotonin crash from their high. This was a new version of a hangover for me. I learned that it wasn't safe to do this drug often for that very reason, but that didn't stop me. Years later, once I'd graduated university and was living in Boston, I continued taking MDMA when I traveled to Prague again and to Miami, California, London, and Italy for music festivals. The first few times of using MDMA had definitely been the strongest and most powerful experiences, but every time after that the effects lessened as my body got used to the substance. Yet I used MDMA multiple times each month just to feel alive. I had grown up believing that getting high or drunk was what living was all about and even the highest expression of life.

In Italy, alcohol was available in abundance, in the form of wine with lunch and dinner. What was even more enticing was that I wasn't twenty-one yet, the legal drinking age in the US. In Florence, I could drink at bars and nightclubs, and I took advantage of this to the fullest. For two euros, I could get unlimited glasses of wine at a sandwich shop across the street from my apartment. Our homestay host, Annabella, would always remark that the trash cans in the bedroom I shared with my roommate were full of wine bottles, making it heavy for her to carry to the recycling.

I had also been psychologically dependent on weed. Drugs make people feel attractive, and I felt invincible when I used weed, which I started smoking during my second year of university, a year before studying abroad. My "big sister" in my sorority loved it, and we were spending a lot of time together. I felt so cool: here was my older friend showing me her ways and teaching me to inhale from a bowl the right way, which took a while for me to get the hang of. Oh, but when I did, I couldn't stop, and it amused me that it had ever been a struggle. We would get high before going to the quad or our sorority events.

All my little anxieties over everything went away with weed. I could handle being high a lot better than being drunk, and there was less of an opportunity for self-destruction. A win-win. But that didn't mean I stopped drinking; I would just mix both. And I began to use drugs as I had used alcohol— in excess. Sometimes I even took the medication Adderall recreationally with alcohol. But those nights I would black out and my heart would race, and I didn't like that. I hated the feeling of the high coming to an end; for someone who felt so out of place in life, the drugs shut off that feeling of not fitting in.

In addition to the drugs and alcohol, I indulged in other unsafe behaviors. Even while living in a homestay with an Italian family, when I studied abroad, I found ways to sleep around, where I got into situations that I wouldn't call "safe." My reckless behavior continued into adulthood, when I lived in London and New York. I would get blackout drunk without meaning to. It felt like, once I'd started, I didn't have an "off" switch to stop. Throughout all those years, I partied hard for fear of missing out. I wanted to experience all there was to experience in life, and I thought that having a good time, being surrounded by strangers, was what *I deserved* and that I was "boring" if I didn't go out most nights of the week. To me, this was living to the fullest, pushing the limits of how far gone I could go. For the longest time, I made an identity out of partying; I thought it made me a fun, exciting badass. I didn't know who I really was or who I could be without a beer in my hand. It would take me years to find the true person inside me.

At Karlovy Lazne, a five-story nightclub that claims to be the tallest, biggest, and most visited nightclub in Central Europe. My friends and I headed there after seeing the group the Glitch Mob at Club Roxy. That was the night that sparked my passion for shows and electronic music.

I chose to brush against other dark aspects of life, too, at university: hanging out in seedy corners of nightclubs until six o'clock in the morning, giving my body away, and spending countless hours at weekend-long music festivals. Even though they seemed like upbeat experiences, the underlying shadow was that we didn't sleep for days by staying awake with drugs. I just wanted to feel wanted; I craved it. While I was drinking most nights, I found myself being a lot more promiscuous than I ever had been in high school. I had a boyfriend the whole time back then, and when I was single in university, I had this void within myself. I didn't feel whole on my own. Combining this feeling with blackout tendencies was a dangerous game. If I was out for the night and my inhibitions were low, a man who was interested in me was my drug. I would feel better about myself for sleeping with someone, even if I didn't remember any of it the next day. It was as though I reverted back to my base human instincts, to connect sexually, when I was under the influence. What so many don't realize—and what I certainly didn't recognize at the time—is that when you are intimate with someone, you give some of your energy away. It's never really no strings attached, at least for me it wasn't. I mistook being loose sexually with empowerment, which is the messaging from society in the media. Casual sex is shown as liberating; it's normalized.

I didn't think this was harmful behavior, because I saw everyone around me doing the same. Everyone I knew was accomplished and smart, so it was the work-hard, play-hard mentality. I just took part in it. Alcohol made it all possible, since I certainly didn't have the courage to be so sexually free when sober.

The dark and destructive aspects of a substance-dependent lifestyle started to give me red flags. In 2014, after a two-day bender of partying, taking MDMA and smoking weed, I had a panic attack the following Monday at work. I had gotten up from my desk too quickly and almost fainted, prompting me to freak out. As discreetly as I could, I called an ambulance to the parking lot of my office. This wasn't the first time I had to be carted away in an ambulance. A year earlier, I had met up with university friends and we each took seven shots before even going to the bar. They were fine, but I couldn't handle it, and one of the boys there called an ambulance for me because I had passed out on the sidewalk. And before then, I broke my collar bone while on vacation in 2011 by jumping on a friend's back while blacked out. I remember the shame, as well as the strain, of having to save up thousands of dollars to pay off the medical bills for multiple ambulance rides. I was carried home and kicked out of more clubs than I can remember for being drunk and incoherent. I'm grateful that nothing worse happened, especially while I studied and lived abroad.

Emotions and alcohol were another toxic combination, but drinking was the only way I knew to deal with my feelings. In New York City, after my dad passed, the mixture of antidepressants and alcohol made my anxiety and depression worse. I was on the edge of a breakdown, when any night out drinking could end with me crumpled in a corner, crying into a friend's arms, with no self-control to stop the emotions from erupting. I knew I was walking on thin ice, and one weekend, when I was visiting my family back in Boston, I shared that I was trying to limit my drinking because it was only amplifying the sadness I was feeling. I made the conscious decision to not drink too much (no more than two drinks), but unfortunately mixing medications (alcohol, drugs, and prescription antidepressants) wound up making me crave them even more. I have always been someone who has stayed true to my word, whether that's to myself or to others, but I wasn't able to fulfill my promise about cutting back. I broke that promise to all of us on one sunny Saturday afternoon, on a rooftop patio in Brooklyn, with friends from work. One glass of rosé turned into two, which turned into three. Then it turned into a whole bottle.

What's one more glass? It's not like I'm out here drinking shots.

The fact that it was wine lulled me into a false sense of security; I had made an excuse for myself to drink. That afternoon, I texted my family in our group text while inebriated. The misspelled words tipped off my family, and they brought up the promise I'd made that I wouldn't drink more than two glasses. When I realized I no longer had conscious control of my alcohol use, I was unnerved, but not enough to stop drinking completely. Something more disastrous would have to happen for me to become more scared.

Another afternoon, I was on the patio of a bar in Brooklyn with friends from work, where someone whom I had just met, Phil, spoke candidly about how he'd realized he was addicted to alcohol, as we all sipped on beers. He said it in a semi-joking way, and I appreciated that he was processing this with us—people he didn't even know well. I think so many of us would benefit from questioning our habits with alcohol, like he did, and his honesty ultimately made a huge impact on me in choosing a different reality.

"So what do you do with that awareness?" Phil asked us. "Go to an AA meeting?"

We all laughed and agreed that would be the most common first step to take. I didn't know it at the time, but when I came to this same realization eventually—that I also might be addicted to alcohol—the seed had been planted for where I could turn.

It was a Sunday, August 7, when I went to a concert at Rockaway Beach in New York with my friend Alyssa from work. The beach was more than an hour-long journey on the subway system. We arrived in the morning around eleven as the band was setting up. We started drinking ciders and sat in hammocks as we waited. This was going to be a day-drinking adventure. As was usually the case when I drank with this friend, we would forget to eat, so enraptured with the act of drinking, chatting, and feeding off each other's energy. We briefly dipped our feet in the icy-cold Atlantic. We took photos of each other basking in the sun and enjoying the music, covers of pop songs. To be honest, by the time the music started, I was already drunk, so I barely remembered it. The music eventually ended around five o'clock, but that wasn't the end of our drinking. Even after the train ride back to the city, my friend insisted we go to her favorite hole-in-the-wall bar in the East Village, and I gladly obliged. I didn't want the buzz of the day to end either. My stomach grumbled on the train ride back, hunger gnawing away on my insides. Alyssa promised there would be food at the bar. Eventually we arrived, around eight. The bar was dimly lit with candles. We started off with a few glasses of white wine, and that was the last thing I remember from that night.

There was no food at this bar, as it turned out—only peanuts that did absolutely nothing to soak up the eight hours of alcohol accumulating in my bloodstream. After just a few glasses of wine for dinner, I blacked out and apparently kissed a middle-aged overweight man. Alyssa had photographic proof.

I woke up in my bed that Monday morning, a workday, with my heart racing. I felt the intense dehydration of having been in the sun for hours without water—the bitter taste and cotton texture in my mouth. Immediately, that familiar sense of dread washed over me as I blinked my eyes. *Shit, shit, shit. What the hell happened?*

I quickly checked my belongings and was relieved to see that I somehow had my phone, wallet, and keys, relieved to find out that the only thing I had lost was my dignity. I had no idea how I could have gotten home, as I searched my Uber transactions on my phone, with no recent rides to account for. I immediately texted Alyssa.

"What happened last night?"

She texted back: "I called you a ride from my phone since yours was dead!" Then she sent some pictures of me with my arm around the middle-aged man with a collared shirt, and I almost threw up.

My drunken antics were typically the butt of my friends' jokes: How could they not be? This time, though, it was too much. I had no recollection, and I was also fed up with playing detective after a night out. I didn't want to have to miss work because of these habits, but I had to take a sick day because I couldn't function. This was the last straw. I cared a lot about my work even if I was struggling with the culture there. I couldn't accept that I was unable to show up at work because what had started as a carefree summer day had ended with an ugly blackout. This was my rock bottom.

That Monday night, on August 8, 2016, I knew I needed to make a change, so I went to an AA meeting nearby, remembering that conversation with Phil at the bar. I needed help. One summer evening in a cold Manhattan church, hearing the speaker's story of his life being completely derailed by alcohol, was enough to shake me to my senses and get me to stop drinking for good.

At Rockaway Beach on the fateful last day I drank alcohol: August 7, 2016.

The drugs and the alcohol worked as an escape—until they didn't. The cons started to outweigh the pros. Sadly, that's usually how addiction goes. At least I was one of the fortunate ones who are able to ultimately see what is happening and make changes before too late. I had grown tired of feeling the inevitable disgrace after drinking and the damage I'd caused to myself and others from it.

Surprisingly, my family couldn't understand why I had stopped.

"Can't you just have one drink?" my mom would ask.

It didn't work that way, unfortunately, because one drink always led to another. It seems that people who enjoy drinking want others to do it along with them, as I would notice with my family and friends who drank.

The gift of making this lifestyle choice was that I could turn to the light, and I could only recognize the light after first knowing the darkness. Darkness can be beautiful in that way. Beginning with the grief from my dad's passing, I had been learning to surrender to a path of healing, which included therapy, meditation, antidepressants, and a plant-based diet. I was becoming increasingly drawn like a magnet to digging deeper into who I was and how I could heal, and I knew these life-giving changes wouldn't gel with my old life-destroying habits. I would now need to eliminate other substances from my life. I began to let go slowly, bit by bit.

Until that August of 2016, I had shoved my grief down with drinking. After I stopped drinking, I ran out of numbing agents and distractions. The grief had a place to well up and be released. Since I wasn't going out clubbing anymore, I was at my New York City apartment more and slowly starting to acknowledge the fact that I was not okay there, in that city. I wasn't performing well at work, and I felt defeated most of the time.

I was getting yelled at, either in person or over email, by colleagues almost daily. It would send shock waves through my stomach whenever I logged on to my work laptop and saw five emails from the manager pointing out everything I had done wrong in previous project emails. Usually, the rest of the team was copied on these emails. I came to the realization that I had been attracting narcissists into my life who behaved in the same way my dad had when he bullied me while growing up. I don't love the term "narcissist," because I'm not a therapist and can't diagnose someone as that, but he, and a manager on my team, definitely exhibited narcissistic behavior.

Narcissism is a personality disorder usually born out of trauma, characterized by a lack of empathy and an inflated ego. Narcissists usually have a low sense of self-esteem, and they hide it by acting otherwise. They are fueled by the adoration of other people, and their fragile egos can be incensed at the slightest remark. After my experience in London, I now began to notice a pattern in my life. I researched healing tools for dealing with narcissism so I could get by at work, which included listening to hypnosis recordings that helped me rewire these patterns.

But I also learned that the reason I was attracting narcissists was due to my own lack of self-esteem. It was a toxic attraction, as if I were emitting sonar that drew narcissists into my life. I was going to have to change how I felt about myself to avoid certain interactions with these types of people and this pattern. At Artel, it wasn't just a single individual's problematic behavior. I learned how companies that don't have systems or values in place to ensure employees are respected will let this abusive behavior run rampant. The culture matters more than the individual in this way. So any personal issues that team members had with me became unresolvable.

Instead of waiting for life to happen to me this time, I decided to take a medical short-term leave for the grief I was still experiencing. I had to find a way to figure out my next steps and get out of yet another toxic environment. At this point, *my* behavior was toxic. I was passive-aggressive, blamed other people on my team for my mistakes, and didn't take accountability for the fact that I wasn't in a role that made the most of my skills and interests. I held all these hurts from my experience in London and was yet again living as a victim. I was a walking open wound.

Cut to December of 2016, after three months on leave from work and alcohol-free. This time allowed me to finally see the light and accept the truth: I was not satisfied at this company or in this city. It was time for my chapter in New York to close, for the sake of my own well-being. I was able to view everything differently without the goggles of alcohol or the perspective of grief.

I was also no longer going out with my colleagues or friends; I still wasn't ready to tell them I had stopped drinking. I was afraid of being judged, because our relationships were centered around drinking. *Would I be rejected if I didn't take part?* I was changing the relationship dynamic, and I was also afraid of my own temptation of wanting to drink by being around them. I knew I would cave, as I'd done in the past.

The slower pace of my home called to me. The anxiety I had in New York had been so crippling—it wasn't until I took a trip home to Massachusetts and went on a hike with my mom and grandma, who was visiting from France, that I realized I was actually able to take full, deep breaths for the first time that week. This moment of acknowledging that I was having trouble breathing, an essential part of *being alive*, showed me that the city wasn't healthy for me. The anxiety I felt couldn't be resolved with a pill or therapy; I needed to make changes in how I was living my life. So I resigned from my job while I was on leave, after putting off the inevitable decision as long as possible. But once I'd made the decision, I had no doubts that

I was doing the right thing. I had set the limit of what I would tolerate, both in terms of how I was being treated and in doing work I didn't care about.

PART 2

Rebirth

CHAPTER 7

Dreamwork

Dreams are the touchstones of our characters.

—Henry David Thoreau

As soon as I quit drinking, my senses opened up to another dimension, on the dream plane, and I started having encounters with spirits in my dreams. When a relationship is so contentious in the physical realm, then once the person passes, it can sometimes be easier to connect in dreams, also known as the astral realm. When my dad passed away, I felt relief from my duties to live up to the expectations of being the oldest daughter. With our family's dynamic, I had been thrust into the role of being a perfectionist and high achiever. I had been the responsible first-born child who was put on a pedestal. The disturbing realization that I had been chasing success for approval from my dad, without even knowing it, had set in. This was a lot of pressure to carry, and I felt bound by responsibility for most of my life. Perfectionism and high achievement are common coping mechanisms for having an alcoholic family member. I was supposed to be a shining example of success for my younger sister, but I toppled off that pedestal after London and New York.

Now that my dad was no longer on the physical plane, I could get a clearer picture of him and who he was, beyond being my dad. I could also let go of some resentment. It wasn't that I now saw him through only a positive lens because he had passed, but I had seen him through such a negative lens for so long that I could now start to uncover some of the redeeming qualities underneath the addictive part of his personality. I started coming face-to-face with his soul in many ways, and this was my introduction into the world of spirits. It's said in shamanism that those experiencing grief are more open to spiritual contact because their barriers to the spirit world are newly open, and this was exactly how I felt.

It started when I got a visitation from my dad in a dream, while I was sleeping in my apartment in New York, before I moved back home. In the dream, I had the clearest sense that he was really there with me, telling me how much he loved me. And that he was okay on the other side. In fact, he shared that he was well! He hugged me, and right afterward, I woke up with a start. I started weeping because I knew what I had experienced was so real yet unexplainable in logical terms.

The first year or so after his death, I was almost like a spirit myself. I felt softer and more vulnerable, as if I were straddling both worlds. In 2017, when I was back in Boston, I felt like I was home and safe for the first time in a long time. But I also felt a little off, in my own world, still going through grief. Unable to put my feelings into words, I spent a lot of time on introspection, and it seemed that, with my dad, a doorway had been opened to the realm of spirits with his presence. I concerned myself more with this world than with the material world, and suddenly career success didn't hold the same weight as it used to. Now that I was connected with someone on the other side, I felt more sensitive and in touch with my emotions overall.

I couldn't really talk to anyone about this at first because I felt like no one would understand. I told my mom and sister, who gave me sideways, nervous glances, which put a damper on my excitement about this connection. I also told my therapist, Derek, who had a different reaction: he was supportive and accepting of what I had to say. He had experienced a similar phenomenon when his parents passed away when he was my age.

Then I got a letter from a close friend, Amy, who had known our family since I was born. This letter was out of the blue; I hadn't spoken to her for years and hadn't seen her since I was in high school. I opened the handwritten, page-long letter, and what I read was further confirmation that my dad was visiting not only me but others in my family's circle as well.

"I had a realistic dream," Amy began, "that I wrote down because, as a creative person, I pay attention to things like dreams and what they mean. In this dream, it looked like it took place in another era, as if it were a black-and-white grainy film. I was standing outside in the rain with your dad, another family friend, and you. We had been at a family party and were now gathered afterward outside, under a streetlamp. Your dad looked like he did when he'd been younger."

This is what spirits choose to do, I would learn, rather than appear as they are when they pass. He had a favorite leather coat from an earlier time in his life, and when I read her description of the coat, light in color and worn out, I knew immediately that her dream was real. He had loved that coat.

Me and my dad; he was helping me bundle up. He was wearing the leather jacket he still wears, in spirit, to this day!

Then she wrote that, in her dream, my dad was trying to tell me that he was right there with me. "But I can't see him, he's not here," I said in Amy's dream. He had his arm around me, but apparently, I was unaware he was doing this. Amy let me know that my dad told her to make sure to let me know about this dream. Amy understood from him that she *absolutely* had to tell me, which compelled her to write the letter to me.

I broke down reading the letter, crying on the bedroom floor for hours. This letter had provided the most healing experience so far on my journey, as it opened up another layer of reckoning for me. It was proof of what I'd already known: my dad was not, in fact, gone. He really was here. He had gotten that message to me through someone else, and this moment was when I realized that sometimes dreams aren't just dreams.

Sometimes our souls travel while we sleep into other dimensions of time and space, where spiritual connection becomes possible.

This is how I started believing in an unseen world that was always around me, even if I couldn't understand it. And I started feeling validated in doing so because, clearly, it was no longer *just me* believing this. I had proof from someone else that my dad was communicating with me. I wrote back to Amy, expressing my gratitude for listening to my dad's message in the dream and for reaching out to me about it. I let her know that it felt real to me, too, even if it wasn't my dream.

Sometimes dreams aren't just dreams.

I've always had vivid dreams, but after Amy's, I started writing down my own dreams right after waking up. Then I would look up the meaning online, on my favorite website, AuntyFlo (www.auntyflo.com), the next morning. I continue to do this even today, and I gain so much insight into the relationships I have with different areas of my life by decoding the symbolism of my dreams. I've also noticed that this dreamwork provides guidance to me on what to do next.

I learned I wasn't the only one in my family who loved interpreting dreams. My mom told me a story about how her grandma, Mamie Jean, would cuddle with her in the morning as a young girl in France and tell her all about the dreams she'd had the night before. It's in my blood, to receive intuitive messages in dreams, just like the women who came before me. That's why I was so taken aback when I felt my mother didn't comprehend my newfound connection with the spirit world.

Sometimes I notice that I feel different after an especially vivid dream, as if something has shifted in me emotionally, and then I have a new outlook about my challenges. Those types of dreams are my favorite. Many dreams have symbolism that is subjective, and I rely on the general meanings of dreams to interpret them in relation to my own life. For example, a few times, I've had dreams about being friends with celebrities. I interpreted these dreams as my subconscious desiring to integrate the qualities of some celebrities, like being talented in their craft, charismatic, and confident. The next day, after these dreams, I embodied these qualities in myself. Changes are happening on a spiritual level during dream time. But some dream elements represent spiritual themes. For example, dreams about the beach, snow, or rain are believed to be all about the purification and cleansing of what no longer serves. These are every-once-in-a-while dreams for me, and when I do have them, they often lead to a powerful transformation in my life.

Dreamwork is an intuitive tool, which can be used for healing and for conversation with your highest self and your psyche. Remember to write down your dream as soon as you wake up, in notes you keep on your phone or in a notebook next to your bed, because you'll quickly forget it soon after you awaken.

Amy's dream marked the start of my new relationship with my dad in spirit, and I had never felt closer to him in my life. It's almost as if, when he was physically here, there had been so many barriers—emotionally, spiritually, and physically—due to his emotional pain and the ensuing addiction. Now, free from those problems, he was present in pure energy form, and I could experience the profoundness of his spirit. I was free to explore a whole new understanding of life and my worldview based on these experiences. And this was only the beginning.

When I saw Derek, who had also been my dad's therapist, it was healing to be connected to someone who had worked with my dad and who knew his intentions had been positive, even if his alcoholism got in the way. I was able to repair my relationship with my dad by working with his therapist, who shared with me how much my dad talked to him about me and different aspects of my life that my dad had been proud of. It was a way of connecting with my dad and of being reassured that he cared for me.

Derek specialized in grief counseling, and he shared that my dad admired how I also had followed my dreams of cultivating a global career, similar to what he'd done. Derek also taught me that it was best to allow grief to be expressed whenever it wanted to. It didn't matter if I was brushing my teeth or if I was driving. Making space for the tears to come up and allowing them to move through me was the best way to heal; conversely, holding in the emotions would make the grief worse. Now I know this is true with any emotion.

Even though I had moved back to Boston and had started therapy, I still took a job that wasn't right for me. Again, it looked good on paper, working for a major telecom client on-site for their marketing communications. This time, it was a much smaller company, and I had thought I could just go back to work and carry on. I'd thought I just needed to switch companies. But it turned out I needed to heal and discover my true purpose. I became burned out, again, because I wasn't doing the right work that made use of my gifts, and I couldn't get excited about my career. Again, I dreaded going into the office and couldn't concentrate. No matter how much I focused on the copy of the email campaigns, making sure they were error-free and sending them to the right email lists, I couldn't get the details right. After this happened a few times, I was put on a performance improvement plan, a repeat of what had happened in New York City. This was my sign: I was repeating another pattern. I couldn't go through the motions anymore; I didn't have the energy for doing this a third time in a row. It was time to take a new path.

CHAPTER 8

Meditation

Meditation is not evasion; it is a serene
encounter with reality.

—Thich Nhat Hanh

Ironically, I had started meditating while I lived in New York.
It was as if the cacophony of the metropolis prompted me to
become quiet and still. A friend invited me to a newly opened
meditation studio called MNDFL in Greenwich Village, and
I immediately fell in love with the space and the practice of
meditation.

It was a refuge from the constant noise all around my
apartment in Midtown East, the loud office where I worked,
and the sound of sirens throughout that electrifying yet
exhausting city.

How refreshing it was to sit down in the secluded studio,
where silence was enforced, and sip organic chamomile tea
while winding down before the guided meditation session. The
lounge was lined with books about mindfulness, blankets, and

live plants hanging from the walls. I learned from wise teach-
ers in the studio how to meditate, and I took my practice back
home with me.

When I left New York and started seeing Derek back in
Boston, I joined a local meditation center he recommended. I
started going to weekly sessions there, and as a member, I was
also able to go and sit on my own, even when there weren't
scheduled events. I began to integrate within the community
as I started attending more workshops and then retreats. I
was ready to face my feelings and be present with all the tur-
moil and uncertainty that swirled within me. I also created a
space in my own home to meditate, with a special pillow and a
reclining memory-foam chair, and I began meditating an hour
each day at home.

I had felt seriously lost at that point in my life, and so many
emotions that I had stuffed down for so long were coming to
the surface. Meditation offered me a respite from the emotional turmoil throughout my first year back home—a place
where I could just *be*, in stillness, and see my feelings from
above, without feeling like they represented who *I was.*

I started to gain more clarity and peace within myself
by going to meditation retreats. One retreat center, in Barre,
Massachusetts, was an hour and a half away from where I
lived, and the only program scheduled during a time when I
could go, in November of 2017, was "The Dharma of Aging:
Equanimity in the Face of Change and Uncertainty." Even
though I wasn't the target audience, something about the second half of the description spoke to me. This was after I had
stopped using both alcohol and drugs and had made other
changes to improve the healthfulness of my lifestyle, and the
title resonated with the uncertainty in my life. I knew I had to
attend.

After checking into the farmhouse, I made my way to the
meditation hall. It was nighttime, and we were gathered in the

most Zen-like place. It was a small, intimate hall with walls of windows surrounded by woods. Inside, it was warm and inviting after the cold November air, and the floor and ceiling were crafted from smooth, polished cedar. The lights were dimmed except for a single spotlight that illuminated a tall, gray Buddha statue at the front of the hall, making the quiet space feel safe and protected. To this day, I have never been in a more exquisitely designed environment that contributed to an overall feeling of tranquility.

I found a cozy blanket and selected a meditation pillow to place on the cedarwood floor. By the time DaeJa Napier, the instructor, entered the room, everyone else had arrived and gathered on pillows, waiting for the evening to begin. This would be a three-day retreat, starting with three hours of meditation on the first night, with a dinner served midway through the session.

The instructor started the session by explaining her background in Buddhist, Zen, and Vipassana meditation practices. She had been teaching for the past forty years. With her straight back, even gaze, and melodic yet deep voice, I admired the dignity of her presence and wanted to emulate it myself.

Over the course of the retreat, I got to know DaeJa well. One day, she dined with me for lunch, and I shared a traumatic experience I had growing up, when I was force-fed meat by my parents when I'd had leukemia. She offered some insight that gave me a new perspective and the ability to forgive my parents. By helping me see their love at the core of what they did, and also the fear they must have felt, I was able to feel and then release my own anger.

I had a notebook for taking notes, and I wrote down something she said on the first night: "Meditation is the most intimate relationship you will ever have in your life." I understood that to mean that being able to be intimate with yourself allows you to have deeper intimacy with others. For so long, I had blocked off intimacy with myself because of pain that was too much to bear. This retreat served as the beginning of getting to know myself and of witnessing my pain so that I could know and accept myself on a deeper level.

The meals provided at the retreat were all vegetarian, and because this was shortly before I had started exploring a diet with a plant-based focus, it was the first time I had eaten this type of cuisine consistently. This would ultimately play a role in how I would eventually change by showing me how grounded I could feel when eating this kind of food, and how easy it is to do so.

Everything about that weekend retreat was an opening to a new level of awareness and peace within myself. I rose early each morning, dressed in my comfiest leggings and sweater, made some herbal tea in the farmhouse, and served myself oatmeal with fruit and maple syrup. I then took my breakfast to an armchair in the lounge, where I looked out the full wall of windows at the backyard, with the winter sun rising over the field behind the farmhouse.

I also admired the maps of the world hung up in the lounge, the Buddhist and Zen artifacts, and the bookcases filled with all this new knowledge I was seeking. I had been so nervous about going alone and not knowing anyone, similar to the fear I had as a child traveling alone, but on the first night, I sat down to dinner and immediately met some welcoming, compassionate people who made me feel at ease right away.

The second day was spent in a talk by DaeJa, followed by a walking meditation outdoors, then a sitting meditation inside. The walking meditation is the one I remember most, because we were given a mantra that we could use along the lines of "I am loving awareness." I must have said this in my mind, and felt it in my body, over a hundred times, as I mindfully picked up and put down one foot and then the other, heel first, on the frost-covered grass. I walked the full expanse of the front and back lawn, all the way to the woods on that cold day. Down by the fruit and vegetable garden, now covered in frost before the winter, I came upon a little maze of rocks and walked into it as I slowly repeated "I am love; I am loving awareness."

I was one of two younger people at the retreat, but I honestly barely noticed any difference between the older people and me. Growing up, I had resonated more with older people, so I was able to develop friendships with many of the people there. By the end of the weekend, I felt like I had bonded with everyone.

No matter how challenging it may be, taking vulnerable steps toward what you want in life, or even taking the steps to figure out what you want, is worth it.

I also got a new perspective on life that made me realize how important it is to go after what you want. One man with short gray hair and a thin, lanky build was dissatisfied with how he had led his life.

"I'm turning eighty years old this year. I don't have a positive relationship with my daughter, and I regret that I haven't found the love of my life as I had expected to," he said. "I don't think there's enough time to repair this relationship or find love anymore." He sounded bitter.

I could sense the helplessness in his voice. He looked deceivingly fit; I would have never guessed he was as old as he was, based on how he was dressed in a knit sweater and athletic-looking pants, but he made it clear he was in a home for the elderly. I decided at that moment that I didn't want to feel like this man, to look back and realize I hadn't done what lit my soul on fire and served others or taken a chance on love. The pain I registered from him was enough for me to realize that no matter how challenging it may be, taking vulnerable steps toward what you want in life, or even taking the steps to figure out what you want, is worth it. Without taking those risks, you may turn eighty and realize you don't have enough time left in your life to make a change for yourself or a difference for the world. What you want is on the other side of fear.

While at the retreat, I learned that I am not my thoughts or my feelings or even my personality. I developed a new awareness that those aspects are not me, and this freed me from so much suffering and showed me my true nature. The walking meditation, with the loving awareness mantra, pivotally changed how I viewed myself. I was someone so much more expansive than my behaviors might indicate, and that new perspective gave me space to see those behaviors and the ability to choose differently.

I also learned that I had the power to change. I was able to consciously release so much shame from my past that I'd been carrying around from my so-called failures and flaws. I also had been carrying around resentments toward my parents, which I spoke about in this retreat, and I learned how to see things from their vantage point without minimizing the truth that I was negatively affected in some ways. It just showed me a fuller picture and, ultimately, what I needed to let go of as I stepped into this void, toward my new, consciously led life.

I learned from this retreat, too, that when you're in a safe space with people who are also dedicated to their own healing, you can be vulnerable and express the things that you're ashamed of or that you're having trouble forgiving. It's an incredibly powerful way to heal, because you are met with acceptance, love, respect, and often guidance, when this may not have been possible in other scenarios, as in your household while growing up. Connection can be medicine too.

This experience showed me that I was seen and heard and supported. At first, I felt self-conscious, just like I had at those Al-Anon meetings. But at this retreat, I had a need that pulled me to share what I was feeling. The timing and the setting were right, and that need to express myself—to find a light to guide me—pushed me past the fear of rejection or of being seen. When a group of thirty "strangers" all smile back at you and share their words of encouragement and guidance, you know you do matter, and you deserve to show what you're feeling. Their willingness to share vulnerably the challenges they were going through assured me that they were nonjudgmental and open.

Although I still had (and have) a long way to go on my journey, I realize now, looking back, that the overall meditation experience and the vegetarian, high-vibrational food were pivotal in the development of my higher awareness, positivity, enhanced energy levels, and uplifted mood. They set a foundation for what I had been seeking: a deeper level of peace. After the retreat, meditation became an even higher priority in my life. The practice had reset my brain waves and created a new pattern of presence and comfort as my baseline of being. It was no walk in the park, sitting with all the feelings I had been burying inside myself now out in the open, but it was freeing at the same time. I was longing to know myself on the deeper, intimate level that DaeJa had mentioned, and I realized that meditation could help me shift into this more steady and embodied lifestyle.

It was empowering to know I didn't have to be pulled by the whims of my outer world, all vying for my attention. I could have the stability to direct my own energy where I wanted it to go. I could sit with all the messy feelings I had numbed in the past and release them in a safe way. I would no longer need to be susceptible to manipulation or misdirection from others (or even myself); I could be solid and sure within myself.

This was quite literally the opposite from how I was used to dealing with life, and I was ready now to stare life in the face and be with whatever was there. Enduringly and compassionately. I was no longer interested in running away from challenges, because what I had seen with my dad had put my life into perspective. An early end could easily be my destiny if I'd continued down the same path he did. That would be a shame, after surviving cancer, to throw my life away to self-destruction.

With this new sense of freedom, I was inspired to make a visible and external commitment to my new lifestyle. I had toyed with the idea of a tattoo back in university but never knew what to get. This time, I knew without a doubt that I wanted a symbol that represented my ability to get over the crippling anxiety I had been burdened with. I got a sigil, or symbol, of the word "breathe" behind my ear. While I once struggled with even taking a full breath, I was now able to breathe with more ease.

I got the tattoo on November 11, 2017, a year after that momentous retreat. It was another decision I made that individuated myself further from my family, because my mom had always hated tattoos and getting one was going against what she preferred. Shortly after my dad and mom got divorced, my dad got a couple of tattoos that showed his pride in his Scottish heritage. I wasn't speaking with him at the time, but I had seen from photos that one was a Scottish flag and the other was the Lion Rampant, the unofficial flag of Scotland with a red lion against a yellow shield. So it seemed that getting a tattoo was another way of connecting with my dad by how we expressed ourselves.

Even though the tattoo was placed behind my ear and hidden from most, just as my anxiety had been hidden, it represented the inner change that I had made. When I got my training in breathwork facilitation years later, further committing to this concept of "breathe," I realized that it was a message from my past self to my future self. My tattoo showed me that my intuition is always tuned into a universal force, like a radio frequency, that knows the way forward.

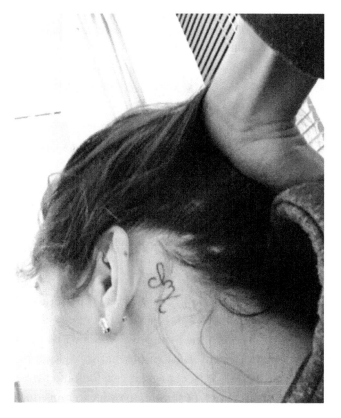

My first tattoo, which I got on November 11, 2017. It's a reminder to breathe. It was a marker of the commitment I made to myself to heal from the anxiety that had been holding me back. It was also a seed that was planted for using breath in healing as part of my future role as a coach.

Now, whenever I feel like I don't know where to turn or am experiencing something confusing or stressful, I turn inward—to my meditation and breathwork practice. Each time I do, I'm still surprised by how much it helps. But it's been most impactful during some of the darkest and most confusing times of my life, as I sifted through the aftermath of decisions I had made that led to suffering. Like how I chose a partner in Asif and let the relationship go on for years, even though I knew he wasn't emotionally available or the best influence. In 2018, it had been two years since I had broken up with him for this exact reason, but I still felt like a fool for betraying myself in this way and for investing my time with him. Meditation was the tool that allowed me to sit with these uncomfortable feelings, to integrate them. It helped me see the gifts from that relationship balanced with the negativity.

And what's surprising is that this practice somehow helps me the most when I'm *not* meditating, because, by visualizing my thoughts and reactions and questioning my behaviors and speech, while sitting in my practice, I make better choices later when I'm out in the world. For example, in other romantic relationships I've pursued, I've been able to more easily notice patterns that I would have missed before, saving me the heartache. My acute awareness comes from the meditation practice.

Sometimes in life, we need to burn down the house and rebuild it from a stable foundation. Sometimes making changes on a faulty foundation in our lives is like just adding new decor to a home that's rotting from the inside out. We don't want to change because we don't want to let go of what we're used to. Then, when we finally decide to change, it can look like we're failing. We might, in actuality, *be* failing, in order to move forward. Sometimes that's the only way.

When I decided to change my lifestyle and career path, it didn't look "successful" from the outside. Success is subjective; it's not something we can let society define for us. My path looked *really* messy from society's standpoint. Boy, was it humbling. But I had to knock down the crumbling building I had lived in and rebuild it in a new and stable way.

Lots of people on the spiritual path experience this. In the first few years of being awakened, I noticed that money was not as readily available to me as it had been before, because I was no longer working in the corporate world with a salaried position. I took temp jobs and freelance work that paid me a fraction of what I had made before I woke up. I had the support of my inheritance from my dad's passing, which was pivotal in making this transition, but after I'd spent the cash, I didn't want to dip into the investments left over. I took jobs that paid enough to cover my basic expenses, and I downsized my lifestyle by living with roommates (even though I dreamed of living on my own) and by saving a lot of money from not drinking or going out anymore.

But I was a different person, and I was becoming clear on the value I offered to the world. I was now occupied with pursuits that didn't have to do with money, and it was like the universe was asking me to focus on those. I had to define myself in other ways than just my job title or how much money I made. My focus was on spirituality and not on what society views as successful. I would no longer accept a career where I was going to burn out, and I needed to honor my new awareness that I was a sensitive and empathic individual.

I worked part-time, and it was the best thing I could do to get back into a relatively "normal" work environment. I had stepped out of the matrix of working for a corporation or Fortune 500 company. With the help of my therapist, Derek, I realized that being in a low-stress job, in the right environment, was best for my reentry into the workforce. I tried some things that didn't pan out, like working in a grocery store for twelve dollars an hour, which can work well for some, but for me was just as stressful as my previous job. I tried dog walking, which was also stressful because I had never owned a dog and now had to walk five at once! But these trial runs led me to part-time work helping family friends who ran their own business. I supported their blog and marketing activities, and in doing so, I witnessed people who had created fulfillment on their own terms, through their own passions and purpose. From there, I moved on to freelance writing for individuals who had successfully built thriving online publications, and it was the first time I was paid for something that didn't feel like work to me. I just followed what seemed right for *me*, and I continued to do part-time gigs until I was influenced enough from these gigs to launch my coaching business.

CHAPTER 9

Stripped Bare

Courage starts with showing up and letting ourselves be seen.

—Brené Brown

I never expected to start my own business. It all happened intuitively, and it took a while for me to get clear on what the business was going to be about. But in the summer of 2017, I became aware that this was my next step. After a few months of going to the meditation center, I noticed there was an alternative-healing center next door.

I looked up the center when I got home one night after a sit and saw they offered astrology, reflexology, acupuncture, massage, and Reiki, which is a Japanese energy-healing tool that uses universal life-force energy to promote healing on mental, physical, emotional, and spiritual levels. As a powerful source of light energy, Reiki can help you get clarity on what is missing in your life. I was intrigued by Reiki, because I was diving deep into the spiritual world by then and wanted to find balance in my body. I booked a session with a woman who drew me in for some reason because of her website, and I thought I'd resonate with her.

It was a humid afternoon in August, but inside, a cool stream of essential oils flowed from a diffuser in the air-conditioned room. I instantly felt at ease, as I took a seat in an upholstered chair directly facing the practitioner, Lauren. She asked me what I wanted out of the healing session. Something about this woman's energy showed me that she really enjoyed what she did for work. I picked up on that, and it gave me a clue that my business was meant to be about helping others, using healing and alternative therapies to transform lives. Surprisingly, we spent much of my session talking about how I realized I was meant to start a business but wasn't sure about what. Lauren said she could see me being a successful business owner, specifically a coach. It's funny how people view you and reflect back what you are sometimes unable to see in yourself.

At the end of the session, as I was walking out, I noticed a display of brown medicinal bottles. They appeared to contain liquids and had colored labels for each different type, spanning every color of the rainbow. I was intrigued, so I asked what they were. Lauren said they were essential oils, and after giving me some samples, she shared a bit about the company. Funnily enough, some of the ideas I had been considering for a business included distributing essential oils, but I wasn't sure how I could do that. Also, I had not been using oils extensively myself, although I had dabbled with a few, using a diffuser for anxiety while I lived in New York.

I had learned that essential oils help balance your mood naturally, especially if you are not drinking. The oils I saw in her office seemed unlike any other kind I had seen, and in my gut I knew these were of a higher quality than the ones I had previously tried. Later, when I used the wild orange and lavender oils she gave me, to manage the stress of my move from one Brighton apartment to another and to help me fall asleep at night, a light bulb went on. These oils *worked*.

They were so simple yet effective. I reached out to Lauren via email a couple of weeks later and asked her for advice on starting a business in holistic healing. She provided a resource for an herbalism course and suggested that the distribution of essential oils would be a great opportunity for me, as would a health-coaching certification. I didn't know much about coaching, but I set out to learn.

Around the same time that I attended the life-changing meditation retreat, I started to get clarity about my professional path. For months prior, I had been exploring many aspects of starting a business. It was an iterative process, where I researched ideas to see if they would be viable. There were so many choices, so I read books and watched free videos on YouTube to get some clarity. I'd originally thought about doing graphic design, so I followed that thread by telling the people in my life about this interest. I got connected with friends of friends who were graphic designers. I took a course on Adobe graphic design software. Overall, I learned it would take more schooling to have a career in this field, and I didn't enjoy it enough for that.

I was more drawn to coaching. The part that felt alluring to me was helping someone make difficult transitions in their life through transforming themselves and believing in themselves again. This profession drew on my gifts of being an empath, or someone who has the ability to tune into another's emotions. With this gift, I could see where someone was stuck, and I could support them by meeting them where they were at. I just had to get over the major resistance I was having to believing I could be a coach.

But I did believe I could help people who had gone through similar life experiences, and I remembered the psychic who had been giving readings at my high school graduation celebration.

The psychic told me I would be a counselor for my career, help-ing other people through difficult experiences. At the time, I thought that couldn't be right, because I was going to school for business and I even wanted to go into fashion. What I hadn't realized back then was that I'm naturally empathic and able to support others and be there for them in their times of need. I hadn't seen how that would give me purpose or what career path that could look like.

At this point, I was able to draw on the past experiences of moving to London and New York to find the courage to take another risk. And this was critical, because risk-taking is a key, necessary skill in entrepreneurship. As the saying goes, there's no reward without risk.

I started by earning my coaching certification at the Integrative Wellness Academy in an online program. It laid a great framework for how to coach clients in a holistic way, looking at all parts of their lives as affecting one another. The course gave me permission to be my own healer. Yes, I could be a coach working with clients, but ultimately I would be a resource, leading that person, like a tour guide, to their inner road map, to be *their* own healer, while I continued along my own healing path at the same time. Doing the work on myself consistently would allow me to hold space for others to do the same. I realized then that I wanted to help people in the same way, healing what holds them back and connecting them to their purpose and intuition. Helping people relieve inner tur-moil, find a sense of balance within, and direct their life paths with clarity, by healing, was what I was going to do.

As I was having this realization, I started gaining more authority over my own life. I had been seeing my family ther-apist weekly for almost all of 2017, and I found I was running out of things to say in the sessions. We had focused on grief, which had helped immensely, and we had talked about career, but I didn't have Derek's support in starting my business. To me, therapy has to be for a specific purpose, and if that purpose gets lost, then the benefit gets lost as well. Once I got to a steady place in my healing from grief, therapy wasn't necessary for that. But my therapist wanted to still see me weekly, although I realized I was just rehashing the same stories. If therapy is used in this way, I believe it doesn't improve quality of life.

At the same time, I had begun incorporating more alternative therapies into my lifestyle. I had been researching how to boost mood naturally, and everything I found pointed to a diet that relied on plants for proteins, eliminated animal-based products, and significantly cut back on processed foods or foods with added sugars.

I was trying to get closer to how I really felt without therapy or mind-altering substances. *Who might I be without any chemicals altering me?* I had no clue, but I was willing to find out, and I was also willing to feel better than I had ever felt before. I already felt more emotionally balanced than I had for a long time. Even when I started to realize that I no longer needed therapy, I put off the decision for a while because I knew it was not what my therapist wanted for me.

I texted him: "Derek, I feel I'm in a healthy place now being home in Boston, and don't need to see you anymore. Thank you for everything."

He responded: "I don't feel comfortable with that. If you're taking medication, you will need to see me, and I want you taking medication."

"Then I won't be taking medication anymore," I wrote back.

He texted: "Then I won't be able to see you ever again, and you'll be receiving a letter from me outlining this."

I guessed this was standard protocol, but it felt like a slap in the face. I had to trust that this was happening for a reason, that Derek had been a support for me in a season of my life, and because I had changed, the universe was showing me it was time to move on.

Derek had mentioned how you had to taper off Zoloft—you couldn't stop cold turkey—and because he didn't give me specific directions, I had to find out online how to do it myself. I was feeling a lot better being home in Boston: I felt settled and also stripped bare of burdensome expectations in my career. I was using a holistic tool kit, so I was ready to stop taking the medication. I tapered off the Zoloft, even though I knew Derek did not agree with this decision. But I realized it was my choice, not his. That was okay with me.

I was doing things for myself now, even if it upset others. I had taken my power back. I had always seen taking medication as a temporary fix. I was in a place where I could heal the pain from my past and not be distracted. So no more antidepressants for me, at least for the time being. I had some side effects like "brain zaps" and nausea, but ultimately the transition was smooth.

By the end of 2018, I wasn't taking any prescription medications, because I finally felt well enough not to. I'm not advising anyone to quit medications they take. I do believe that finding alternatives while still taking medication and then seeing what's helping *before* coming off a prescription is a wise course of action. I've gone on antidepressants since that time, when the alternatives have not been enough, since my sensitive disposition teeters on the edge of anxiety and depression. I'm in tune with myself when my life circumstances change, and I go back on them when needed for a period, under a doctor's care. There's no shame in seeking support by using these medications, as they can truly give some people their lives back.

When I was no longer relying on pharmaceuticals or illegal drugs, I began to take whole-food-based herbal supplements, use essential oils, and eat a whole-food/plant-based diet. I practiced breathwork and kundalini yoga. I also regularly journaled, meditated, prayed, read spiritual texts, and hiked. In addition to all the other lifestyle changes I had been making, I also stopped using chemicals found in personal products and makeup on my skin. I only used nontoxic cleansers and moisturizers from the essential oil company dōTERRA, because I knew that they were free from fragrances, as well as other chemicals that are harmful. I quit wearing makeup altogether in 2018.

An added side benefit of eliminating makeup from my life was that it allowed me to be seen for who I was, without a mask. I truly didn't care any longer what people thought of me; I just wanted to be laid bare. I stopped wearing jewelry, and I didn't make any effort with my hair. Before, I always made sure my hair was straightened or curled or styled in some way. Instead, I cut it chin-length and just blow-dried it or even let it air-dry. I donated my corporate wardrobe, and I didn't buy any new clothes. I wore leggings and plain T-shirts most of the time.

In other words, I let go of the pressure I'd felt as a woman to do all these things to be accepted or presentable in the patriarchy. As I write this, I'm just starting to get back into makeup and clothing, and I'm getting creative with my new style. So that I feel beautiful, for me. I know now that I'm beautiful without makeup, and I use it to accentuate my features when I feel like it, rather than applying it every day to cover up my face and its imperfections or to look presentable for society, for women or men.

My whole mentality changed with this process of cleaning up my body and my lifestyle. I felt perfectly confident without makeup, and later on I also invested in plant-based, cruelty-free vegan makeup. No longer willing to put toxins on my body, I wouldn't have to feel the effects of all those chemicals compounding daily.

As I started to detox from all the toxins I had been putting in, and on, my body, every one of my senses started to revive

after being dulled for so long. I could feel the summer breeze
flow against my skin and through the hairs on my arms, and I
began to notice how aromatic the lily of the valley was along
my walking path. Clear ideas about what to write in this book
dropped into my consciousness as I crossed the street and reveled in the pink sun setting. I was also able to open up my heart
again after it had been closed down for so long because of the
grief I had experienced.

Healing involves removing a lot of unhealthy things first, before becoming.

My psychic senses, which had been dormant since childhood, started to come back online, with full force. They had
been buried under all those toxic habits and self-deprecating
beliefs for so many years. Healing involves removing a lot
of unhealthy things first, before becoming. I started seeing
visions in my mind, my third eye, that would give me messages
on what I should do next with certain life decisions. I'd mostly
see animal spirits pop up in my mind's eye and would look to
that animal's behavior and qualities to inform my next steps.
For example, if I saw a turtle in my mind, I would take it to
mean I should be patient and slow with my decision, taking the
time to review all the choices available.

All humans have intuitive abilities, and I learned that the
more you practice becoming aware of them, the stronger they
become. It was divine when I met the Reiki practitioner who
went on to mentor me in my business. As an intuitive medium,

she was able to help me realize that I had a sixth sense, or superpower, that was starting to awaken. I trained with her in a Reiki Level 1 course for the sole purpose of activating more of my intuitive abilities.

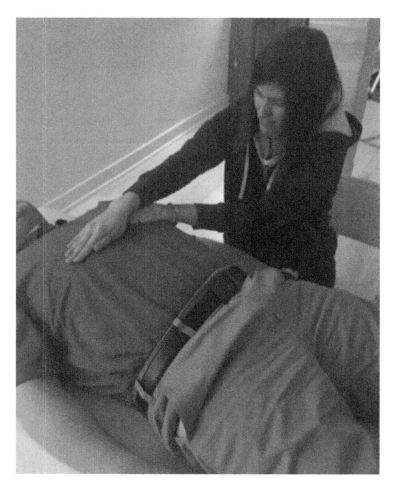

Giving Reiki during my level-one training, which connected me to my intuition.

The first time I'd dreamed about my dad, after he passed, was a visitation, and the second time he visited me was through my family friend's dream. I'd wanted to believe he was connecting with me, but I had grown up in a nonbelieving family that didn't acknowledge the spiritual world or have a religious practice. My mom had grown up Catholic, going to church every weekend, but she didn't want anything to do with the church after it was forced on her during her upbringing. And I had been educated by a school system and city that focused on science. So with that background, it was pretty hard for me to believe, at first, that I would have any intuitive abilities.

But now I wanted to learn more about how to use my supernatural skills so that I could contact my dad again. I finally had my own experience, in a personal development workshop, where I contacted him.

CHAPTER 10

Psychic

I shall not commit the fashionable stupidity
of regarding everything I cannot explain as a
fraud.

—Carl Jung

I wonder how much more powerful we could be if we didn't
have toxins clogging our bodies and beliefs. Why are we
pumped full of toxins from the major conventional brands
in our society? Is it to keep us disconnected from our innate
powers? And what might happen if we could believe in things
beyond what can be scientifically proved? What if we all woke
up to our extrasensory powers and used them to make better
choices? It's much harder to control thriving, spiritually connected, self-sufficient, and educated people than those who
are obedient, drugged, and unconscious. I believe toxins are
meant to disconnect us from our powers. That's why detoxify-
ing your lifestyle contributes to a more honest life experience,
and allows you to connect with your true essence.

I dabbled with a lot of intuitive courses to see which ones would resonate. I tried a shaman circle, a general intuitive development class, and then a mediumship development group, just to name a few. I had already been going to different types of psychic development circles for a while, and I felt my senses getting stronger. The fact that mediumship is all about connecting with the dead intrigued me, because I could talk with my dad this way. Because he had passed away at a time when I hadn't been talking with him, I felt like there was so much more to say. So much I didn't know about him. And I knew he was trying to reach me this way somehow, especially after Amy's dream.

I attended a mediumship circle for the first time at Circles of Wisdom, a metaphysical store that was forty-five minutes north from where I lived in Boston. On a blisteringly cold winter morning, I showed up wrapped in my scarf and kept my coat on as I took a seat in one of the folding chairs of the wide circle, at the center of the chilly room. Still, I was open to whatever was going to happen.

We started by introducing ourselves and sharing why we had come to the group. The young man sitting next to me, Alex, had messages for me about my dad. I didn't say anything at first, when Alex said he had heard an accent, although this did tip me off, but then he said the spirit's name was Graeme. I was flabbergasted to hear this name come out of his mouth. I turned to him.

"That's my dad."

Alex said my dad was almost yelling at him to be brought in so he could speak to me, and I knew that was the classic angry Scotsman my dad was. No doubt. He told Alex he was trying to talk to his "baby girl," and although I was quite embarrassed at first, I recognized his nickname for me, his way of calling me, so I knew this was for real.

Now here is where it got even more interesting. Spirits don't always speak directly with words; they use images to convey messages too. This is known as clairvoyance, when someone can receive these images as messages. Like me, Alex was also pretty new to intuitive development, and he started to share the images he was getting.

First, he described seeing suitcases and boxes being packed and moved. This could be interpreted in many ways, I learned, as people in the circle chimed in with their insights. Some said it could be taken literally, like an impending move, or it could figuratively mean it was time for me to remove the baggage I'd been carrying from the past. In both ways, this image resonated with me.

Alex also shared that he could see oranges and my dad drinking orange juice, which some people in the group said could be related to healing one of the chakras, which is an energy center in the body. The sacral chakra, located below the belly button, is a center for creativity and sexuality and is represented by the color orange. Then, just as suddenly as this message came through, Alex said he lost contact with my dad because he had become so focused on figuring out what the images were, getting stuck in his mental mind. I wasn't upset, though. I was satisfied, because I knew it was my dad, and it was getting easier to connect as I was learning more too.

The second time I went to this mediumship development group, I connected with my dad in a different way. The group started with a meditation led by the teacher, which primed us to connect with spirits. We then split into partner groups to channel for each other. This was different from the first session, where it had been an open group reading.

We counted off to be assigned in pairs. I sat in a chair facing a lovely older woman, Claire, and we began to get to know each other before the reading started. We had so much in common: she was also a life coach, had overcome a dark past, and was an artist.

We were each going to bring in a spirit for the other person and convey what messages we received. As I still felt like I had no idea what I was really doing, I wasn't expecting much and told my partner the same. I was open to whatever was going to show up, but I wasn't even sure *how* to receive messages from a spirit, and in truth, I just didn't think I would.

I was first up, and as I closed my eyes, I surprisingly started to see images inside my mind. The first image I got was of an older woman in an old house. It was almost as though I was walking through the house and going through the rooms. I asked if this sounded familiar. Claire said it could be her sister, who had passed, but she wasn't sure.

Then I saw a mixing bowl and pans set out. When I shared this, she said she often baked with her sister at their family home and that I was seeing her sister! That was all I got, and I honestly couldn't believe how I had been able to see these things and connect with a stranger's spirit. It was the first time I had done anything like this, and I believed the beginning meditation must have opened something up for me, because this was wild. It was better than what I had expected.

What happened next was nothing short of a supernatural phenomenon, and it reflected what I had already known to be true: my dad was on the other side and communicating with me.

It was Claire's turn. She said she could see a man who was thin and wearing a worn-out leather jacket and shorts, with longish flowing hair. That leather jacket again tipped me off right away. I was confused about the longer hair and thin build, so I told her that I knew my dad to be round and have a buzz cut.

"Spirits choose what age they want to look like, when they felt best," she said, confirming what I had learned when Amy had sent me that letter describing her dream with my dad in his favorite worn leather jacket from when he was younger. This makes sense; I would want to look my best in the afterlife too, so I'm glad to hear there is the option.

Then all of a sudden, Claire's breath caught and she started tearing up, then crying.

"What's wrong, what's happening?" I asked.

"Your dad loves you, and it's so overwhelming, this feeling of love. It caught me off guard." This, of course, moved *me* to tears.

Another way that spirits communicate with us is through feelings. This is called clairsentience; basically, spirits will send a feeling as the message. People sensitive to these energies, like myself, can sometimes feel out-of-place emotions, out of the blue.

As she started telling me more of what he was saying to me, she burst out crying again.

"I love Emily so much," my dad said through her. "I realize how much I messed up, and I know I can never take that back, but I'm sorry and I love her so dearly, and always have."

Claire could not have known this, as she wasn't at the previous circle when my dad had been channeled by Alex. She explained that spirits don't hold on to regret or pain, like humans do, but that doesn't mean they aren't aware of damage they've caused.

"That was so moving to hear because I did not always feel that love from him when he was alive," I said.

My dad had his own unresolved issues with his upbringing, which he had unconsciously passed down to me and which I'd internalized as a child, not feeling worthy of my dad's love. This had manifested, in later years, as choosing partners who were emotionally unavailable and in tending toward perfectionism, needing to achieve success to validate myself. This was ultimately why I broke up with my ex, Asif, at the start of 2016: as a Muslim he was not allowed to be with me. In fact, I had been kept a secret from his family for the year that we were together. This wound ran deep.

Through my partner in this circle, I was able to feel what my dad's true spirit had realized and what he'd resolved within himself, and the experience immensely helped me heal from that destructive belief I had held about myself for most of my life. It also brought healing to the relationship I had with my dad.

This is when intuitive development started to feel like magic for me: when the people in these groups who connected with my dad's spirit were able to tell me things about him that only I knew, like how he called me "baby girl" or how he loved his leather jacket. It was undeniable. I became a believer, but with a dose of skepticism, I would add. It's really easy for people to claim they are psychic, and I came across a handful of these people, but most practitioners I met in practice groups were honest.

My dad also told me, through Claire, that he was so proud of me for starting my own business and that he could see my entrepreneurial spirit.

"He's showing me a notebook with a pen," she said. "I believe this shows that you need to keep writing, and that what you write is powerful."

In some ways, this book is a reflection of me taking his advice and moving forward with my writing. Interestingly enough, the next time I "met" my dad was at a workshop called "Writing from Life," facilitated by Allan G. Hunter, at a friend's creative and personal growth studio—the same studio where I would later show my artwork. In that workshop, we learned how writing was "soul" work that would lead to healing for us and for the people who encountered our work. That really hit home for me, and I realized that may have been part of the reason my dad had been nudging me to write.

We also took part in a shamanic-journeying type of meditation at the workshop, which allowed us to access our subconscious minds and the spirit world. We were asked to visualize that we were walking along a path and to see if we saw someone up ahead whom we couldn't recognize at first. The person became clearer as we got closer, and for me, it was my dad. I was walking on the cliffs in his hometown of Arbroath, Scotland, where his ashes are scattered. Then we were asked to visualize this person pulling something out of a bag.

What he pulled out of his bag was a leather-bound notebook and a pen. Another clear sign that I was being guided to write this book was that my dad made sure to share this message with me at any chance he could get. I listened to my dad's urgent messages and committed myself to the writing, and the healing, of my soul.

CHAPTER 11

Inner Child

In all chaos there is a cosmos, in all disorder a
secret order.

—Carl Jung

I had already been trying different healing modalities, such as
acupuncture and spiritual energy healing, when I read the book
*The Emotion Code: How to Release Your Trapped Emotions for
Abundant Health, Love, and Happiness* by Dr. Bradley Nelson.
I learned that emotions from traumatic events can get lodged
in our bodies if we never deal with and release them. I used the
healing processes outlined in the book to pinpoint my different emotions and beliefs at the ages they occurred throughout
my life thus far.

By this point in my journey, I had reached the dark night of
the soul stage of my awakening. I felt so much suffering coming up from everything I had never healed from, and I had no
more crutches to lean on—no alcohol, no drugs, no prescription meds. Most people believe that a spiritual awakening is

a serene, illuminating experience, which it certainly can be, but it's typically preceded by the exact opposite type of experience. A dark night of the soul is a spiritual experience, even though it may feel like intense depression, anxiety, and emptiness and could even lead to suicidal ideation. For me, the dark night of the soul manifested as a period of wrenching despair and aloneness, when I became aware of the dysfunctional family dynamics that had affected me, as well as every role I had played in my own suffering.

I learned that I was catering to the ego needs of my family—of being the person they needed me to be to serve *their* interests and to match *their* perception of who I was. This is when I became aware of my own trauma, and the trauma of the world I lived in. I had flashbacks of painful memories from when I was a child that I had long forgotten. In my training as a coach, I learned that virtually everyone has experienced trauma, because we live in a traumatized society. Our family's generational trauma is passed down to us as well. There is such a thing as a "small t" trauma, and it is just as impactful as a "big T" trauma. It's helpful to understand your pain through this lens and to give it respect in this way. Sometimes we might feel that if nothing extreme happened to us physically or emotionally and if we were well provided for by thoughtful parents, we haven't experienced trauma. But as someone who has experienced trauma on varying levels, I can say that both big T and small t traumas can affect us in similar ways. It's our reaction to an event that defines the nature of trauma. Trauma caused me to form a limiting belief about myself and my perception of the world, which then caused me to act however I needed to so that I could prevent that trauma from happening again.

During this period, which lasted a little over a year (but was like an eternity at the time), I felt so isolated, because I couldn't put into words what I was going through and feeling, and I knew no one around me would understand. I cried a lot, slept a lot, and experienced spontaneous explosions of emotion. I generally felt off. I couldn't hold down a full-time job, and I was grateful for the privilege of having my dad's inheritance as a financial resource. For the first time in my life, I didn't have to focus on making money at the expense of my own well-being. It felt, in a sense, as if my dad was supporting me on my path of deep healing in this way.

A part of me, my old personality before the awakening, was dying, and I was mourning it. So much anguish from my past was being released because I was now in a safe place to heal it. I was out of the rat race and acclimating to a new, more sustainable way of living, without burning out. Financial collapse can also be part of the dark night of the soul, and in one way, I was losing that connection to making money because I had to learn to feel secure in myself with or without it. I lived minimally and stopped buying clothes, going on trips, and spending money going out. Even though I had a financial cushion, I still felt the unsettling disconnect of not tying my worth to my ability to generate income.

After six months in 2018 of struggling to build my business and to find work that matched my previous corporate salary, I started to lose hope. My identity had been wrapped up in my career, so I didn't know who I was without that, and this *terrified* me. I had been, and still was, looking for different ways to transform all this pain into peace so I could move forward. That's what made me open to trying different therapies—I was still searching for the one that could help me the most—and I was willing to try anything that would take this pain away. People usually come to a spiritual awakening because they have either a distressing crisis or a hollow feeling that doesn't go away until they address it.

Once I started becoming more conscious of the toxic patterns I'd been repeating in my career and through my addictions, and began changing my lifestyle choices, I was ready to look at past experiences I hadn't been ready to look at before, from my upbringing and later. *What had happened that drove me to such a devastating need to escape?*

There were many areas that contributed to my debilitating beliefs and behaviors, such as my parents' parenting style and my dad's alcoholism. There wasn't just one cause, but I found that the majority of my emotional pain stemmed from when I was three years old and had leukemia. In 2015, I learned for the first time from my primary care doctor in New York City that this was a root cause of the anxiety and other mood disorders I later experienced as an adult. I had been officially diagnosed with acute depression and anxiety when my dad died in 2016, but I had experienced anxiety and depression while growing up. It had just been undiagnosed. Apparently, I had more than just physical scars from that illness, so I started to examine this trauma.

This life-threatening illness required me to spend extended periods of time in the hospital. Because I was so young, the nurses weren't always straightforward with me about my surgery, medications, or treatments. They would distract or even trick me, whenever possible, to avoid scaring me. For example, medicine was snuck into my food, even though I could clearly tell it was crumbled on my ice cream. At home, I'd hide my medication in the couch pillows or throw it in the serving bowls at dinner.

Because my parents and medical providers weren't forthcoming with me, I learned to read their expressions and body language to figure out what was happening. And because I spent a lot of time alone, I could observe others from the vantage point of my bed and try to figure them out. From this childhood belief that others were not always straightforward, I found it difficult to trust people as an adult. I was learning that this lack of trust was an unhealthy coping mechanism.

When I started writing as part of my healing journey, I initially didn't want to write about my experience with leukemia. I thought that writing about it would somehow bring it into my present moment again, and I wanted to forget about that time in my life at first. One of the impacts of my hospital experience was that it contributed to emotional patterns of hostility. One time, after a hospital stay in a room with detailed artwork depicting Disney's Ariel character on the windows, when I returned to the hospital but didn't get the same room, I was incensed. That was "my" room, I thought, and it felt like the one constant thing I had was snatched away. Another time, when one of the nurses bathed me, I screeched as if I were being tortured. I became known as a difficult patient and was referred to as "feisty." I didn't do as I was told. And I especially didn't like being deceived.

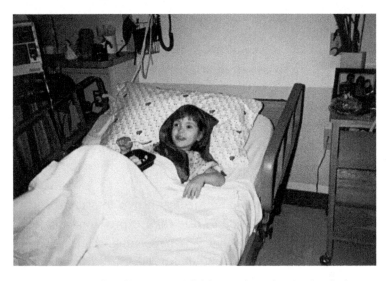

Eating ice cream with medication in it. I didn't want the medication, but the fact that I got to eat ice cream in bed while watching Disney movies made it go down easier.

In addition to the ice-cream trick for delivering medicine, I was once tricked into believing there were "chocolate shoes" under the operating table so that I would lie facedown and still enough for an injection in my back, which preceded my bone marrow transplant. I still remember the feeling of the cold steel on my stomach and the shock of realizing that a needle was piercing the skin on my back. But the "fighters" and difficult patients are more likely to survive cancer, I learned later. I didn't accept my situation, and I'm grateful that this happened when I was younger and less resigned than I could be as an adult.

My parents forced me to eat meat, believing it would support my blood, since leukemia is a blood cancer born from not having enough white blood cells. But I've never liked red meat, ever since I was young, and instead of eating the beef, I'd usually hide it in a napkin and later flush it down the toilet. One night, my family and I had spaghetti and meatballs for dinner. As usual, I wasn't eating the meat, but for some reason, this time my parents didn't accept this behavior. My mom and dad teamed up to physically restrain me, holding my mouth open and pinning my hands behind my back to stuff the meatballs down my throat. It feels daunting to share this dark family secret, but I have learned to forgive them for doing what they felt they needed to do to keep me alive. It shows how fearful they must have been. The most interesting aspect is that my mom felt the same way growing up, hating red meat. She was forced to eat all sorts of meat as part of French cuisine, such as blood sausage, beef tongue, and rabbit. She'd hide it, too, to avoid eating it, and it seemed to me that she was just repeating the pattern of forcing meat, from her own childhood, because it was what she knew. That's what parents do if they don't become aware and choose differently, by doing the work to unravel these patterns.

In the hospital, I shrieked at the nurses for just *walking* by my hospital room, because I'd learned that I couldn't really know what would happen next. Better to prevent them from coming in, just like a dog barks to protect its territory. Much later, in my healing, I discovered that my issues with trust and betrayal were the result of this early childhood experience and that this pattern of hostility had a name, transference. My tempestuous energy would trigger the nurses, perhaps reminding them of an instance in their own childhood when a parent yelled at them, and in response, they would react with petulance toward me. It was no secret that I didn't like the nurse assigned to me, and it was because I experienced this unconscious reaction of indignation. Transference is when you can't see someone clearly, and you instead associate them with someone else in your life who reminds you of a painful memory. It's typical in therapy and coaching for transference to occur, and it's also an opportunity to heal that relationship with the person whom it's serving as a reminder of.

The feelings of mistrust and betrayal that I developed at that young age were compounded by all that time I was alone in the hospital, which affected my attachment style. Being separated from my parents made me think I was not worthy. At that age, we are all completely ego focused, and I took it as rejection when my parents wouldn't stay overnight at the hospital with me. I remember being awake at night, with *The Lion King* soundtrack playing through the speakers in the ceiling, having to rely on that comforting lullaby to sing me to sleep without my parents. The hospital's fluorescent lights and the rooms within the Dana-Farber Cancer Institute, part of Boston Children's Hospital, were similar to those of a corporate office building, and I believe this similarity triggered my hostility in my corporate career.

These challenges in my childhood enabled me to develop and hone some important skills. I learned to read people, my

perception skills allowing me to detect a change in voice into-
nation or a shift in energy that would tip me off to what would
happen next. I developed an ability to use all my senses instead
of just my logical mind. I did this for survival in those hospital
times, but these abilities were further developed as I grew up
in my family home and later in my adult relationships. I view
them now as inherently part of me, as my greatest assets when
guiding others in my one-to-one sessions, and as skills I regularly use in my daily life. They allow me to grasp a fuller picture of people and situations and to relate better with others by
matching their body language and meeting them where they
are on an emotional level.

I went through a similar dark night of the soul when I was
a child, because I had to rely on pure faith to get through leukemia treatment. Cancer patients often have a spiritual experience, because they have to be completely present, unsure if
they have the next minute, or next month, to live. They can
develop a faith in some force that wants them to be alive or die;
it's left up to fate. Some patients choose to make the most of
the time they have because they don't know if they'll have the
opportunity to live another day.

In *You Can Heal Your Life* by Louise Hay, she attributes
an emotional root cause for every type of physical pain and
offers affirmations to shift the pain from an internal standpoint. This led me to contemplate whether there had been an
emotional root cause underlying my childhood illness. Was it
possible that I had leukemia because I felt ignored by my parents, during their tough transition moving to a new country?
Could this emotion have manifested as physical disease to get
their undivided attention?

I was still seeing Derek at this time, and he had a slightly
different spiritual perspective from mine. He suggested the
concept of a soul contract and the idea that I had subconsciously decided to go through this leukemia experience as a

key learning in my life. With his input, I adopted a new concept, which was later reinforced in my integrative coaching training: always isn't always, and never isn't always never.

Situations are fluid and subjective, and a one-size-fits-all approach may not always apply. In my case, maybe the physical disease didn't initiate from an emotional root. But in looking at this experience through different lenses, I learned how to question my beliefs and how to be flexible with them.

This opened me up to another concept: the idea that we have an inner child who is always with us, even as adults. I had buried my inner child a long time ago, when I grew up in the traditional schooling system and, later, when I went to university. I said goodbye to that carefree and curious part of me who loved to be unencumbered and creative when I entered university after the recession that began in 2008. At that time, I believed I needed to choose a degree that would yield a return on my investment and lead to a stable career so I could pay off my loans.

Always isn't always, and never isn't always never.

I was all too aware of the sacrifices my parents were making for me to go to the private university of my choice, and I wasn't going to mess that up. My family had hoped that I would commute to a state university because of my dad's unemployment at the time. But I wanted to do well, not only for myself but because I knew what was at stake if I graduated without a job during that recession. So I decided to go to Bentley University and earn a marketing degree.

Let's say *carefree* and *creative* were not part of my vocabulary at all by then, but they really hadn't been for a while, maybe even since 9/11 in 2001. I was only in elementary school at the time, but as an empathic child, I realized, along with so many others, that the illusion of a perfect, harmonious world was shattered that day. That event caused the world to realize that darkness does in fact exist. It was out in the world for all to see, no longer able to be ignored.

All this is to say I've learned so much about myself in recent years through my willingness to examine why I am the way that I am. I've also come to terms with the decisions I made when I was in survival mode. They led me to where I am today, after all, so they did serve a purpose. My inner child was a little lost for a while, but this is not uncommon in our capitalist society.

I learned that your inner child is always with you, and if you don't consciously connect with it as an adult, you can unknowingly (and unconsciously) allow your inner child to sometimes run your life. This is as if your five-year-old self is making adult decisions from a place of pain that occurred at that age.

So I started being intentional about connecting to that untroubled, childlike part of myself. I did this by making my favorite childhood dishes, like waffles (I distinctly recall adoring the Eggos with the Batman symbol on them), and watching childhood movies, like *The Lion King* (so traumatizing, though!). I played with children and pets. I painted. I allowed myself to be goofy with friends. It's really easy to lose sight of playfulness and fun in a personal development and spiritual community where we lean more toward the side of seriousness in devotion. I had to actively cultivate these carefree qualities in my healing to connect with the related emotions that were needed for balance within.

After having fun with that for almost a year, I then started connecting with my inner child through visualizations and meditations. I practiced tapping, also known as Emotional Freedom Technique (EFT), which helps you rewire your subconscious for inner-child healing by tapping your fingers on different energy points on the body while repeating affirmations.

As a healing adult, you can go back and give your child self the love that you didn't receive when you were young. It's so empowering doing this work, because it means it doesn't matter what your childhood was like or how your parents raised you. *You* are the one that can heal your inner child, and *you* have a responsibility to re-parent yourself in the way that you like. Instead of yearning for that stable parenting you never felt you received, and unconsciously seeking it out in your friendships and romantic relationships, you have the power to give it to yourself.

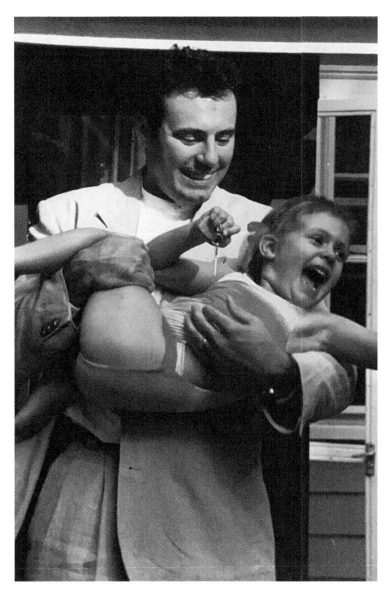

Me at my remission party with the doctor who had treated me. I love knowing that this playful little version of myself is always inside me and ready to connect with when I let life get too serious.

CHAPTER 12

Awakening

> Your vision will become clear only when you
> can look into your own heart. Who looks out-
> side, dreams; who looks inside, awakes.
>
> —Carl Jung

Being asleep, or disconnected from your spirit, is akin to driving down the street and spacing out deep in thought, only
to realize miles down the road that you were unconsciously
driving. It's like moving through life in a wind, letting various people and ideas sway and pull you in different directions
without your choice in the matter. It's looking at what everyone else around you is doing and using that as a guideline for
what you should be doing, wearing, eating, watching, et cetera.
It's looking outside—to the media, to the government, to the
corporation—for directions on what to do. It's a lot easier, in a
sense, being asleep because you can be blissfully unaware. You
can outsource responsibility. But that doesn't mean it's the best
way to live your life.

Being awake means you start to become aware of every-thing, including what is working and what isn't. Awakening shines light on the ugliness of the world and in your own life. It's like turning the lights on in a messy and dingy basement that you've neglected for a decade. You just kept throwing stuff down there, without looking at what needed to be organized or thrown away. Awakening forces you to take responsibil-ity for your life. And it also makes you aware that there are infinite possibilities available to you. Awakening to your own inner wisdom and energy forces you to look inward and see what is going on beneath the hood, so to speak, so that you can influence the external world, instead of being influenced by it. Awakening means taking your power back.

Awakening is like taking off a pair of blurry, dirty, smudged glasses and realizing you can see so much more clearly and have extra senses of perception through your intuition. We are all limitless beings, but we take on faulty ideas, projections of others, and, quite frankly, *lies* about who we are, because that's what our society has been built on—programming. Our chal-lenge is to realize that connecting to a universal loving energy is going to lead us home to ourselves. This is the part of our-selves that's truth, our pure essence within. The rest is lies.

How can we "fail" when we have supportive energy, what-ever we choose to call it: Gaia, god, the universe, spirit, angels, guides, galactic family, earth angels, not to mention all our ancestors. They have all been a part of our births and journeys into this world. We each came here for a reason, and the more we focus on this truth, the more we can embody who we truly are authentically, expressing our light, our soul, our wisdom. Your life can expand when you recognize that unseen forces are conspiring for your growth and becoming.

I realized early in my business that, when I was hiding my gifts because of low self-esteem, I was actually being selfish. I was created so I could bring the healing medicine that only I can offer, through my gifts and experience, and the same goes for each of us. As a coach, I'm a conduit for energy and guidance to flow through. Our ego voices might whisper that there are already enough people out there doing what we're called to do, or that our input doesn't matter. Believe me when I say that this is a lie to keep us small. Starting a business forced me to address my issues and to charge other people for my spiritual gifts, and it wasn't until I hired coaches and healers to help me own my value that I did. I turned to people that had a blueprint for the way forward.

This is a lie to keep us small.

You, too, can awaken to the fire and the eternal energy that exists within you, no matter what your life currently looks like. In order to awaken, you can work to clear what stands in the way of your divine true essence. Know that this unending force will go beyond this life—this space and time—so you need only focus on expressing your essence as it wants to be seen and heard right now. On your journey, you will unlearn a lot of what was taught to you through societal programming and through your upbringing, and then you will get closer to the truth and awaken to who you truly are. You are more than worth it. You were born to awaken, to remember your true nature.

CHAPTER 13

Discernment

Believe nothing, no matter where you read it, or who said it, no matter if I have said it, unless it agrees with your own reason and your own common sense.

—Buddha

I first woke up, and became aware of the matrix, when I was in London. This bustling metropolitan lifestyle was the first experience to show me that everything I had been taught to believe about success and the ego-driven lifestyle was an ideal put out into society. That ideal worked for some, but not for many. I lost the identity I'd thought I had when I was fired from that job. It felt like a part of me had died, my ego, which was built on lies. I was reborn but didn't know it.

My second awakening was when I had my heart cracked open through grief when my dad died and I was living in New York. I took action and opted out of the system by moving back to Boston, without a plan on what to do next.

The third time was when I heard about the mass shooting in Las Vegas in 2017; it was the largest in the US at the time. It was not the first tragedy of this kind, but it was the first time I felt something was off in the story that was being portrayed on the news. It wasn't adding up, with the timeline being changed multiple times by the police, and I didn't believe the messages the media were putting out. The official story was that the gunman, Stephen Paddock, acted alone, raining bullets down on a crowd at the Route 91 Harvest music festival. Yet the shooter had frequent help from hotel bellmen, as he brought five suitcases to his room on September 25, seven on the next day, two on September 28, six on September 30, and two on October 1. Would this not spark any suspicion from security? His collection of weapons included fourteen AR-15 rifles, eight AR-10-type rifles, a bolt-action rifle, and a revolver. Was one person shooting all of these rifles and able to kill 58 people and injure 867 others? Skepticism was rife because not enough details were shared about the shooter himself or the incident. Other questionable details included a twenty-five-year-old Mandalay Bay security guard named Jesus Campos, who was a key witness in this tragic event and who first encountered the shooter. He fled the country to Mexico almost immediately afterward, skipping most of his live TV interviews, which could have shed more light on the incident. Soon after, the story disappeared from the news, and I never heard any more in the media about it. What this tragic event did for me was two things.

One, it forced me to deepen my faith in a higher power. That was the only way for me to move forward after hearing about a mass murder this tragic. And two, it encouraged me to be more discerning about the world around me, as well as the people around me, and to not take any information at face value. Even spiritual information. It didn't help that, at a time with a vacuum of information, theories of what had happened—including witnesses' personal testimonies—were censored and taken down from YouTube. Basically, anything that didn't line up with the official narrative was removed, which led to further speculation. Overall, my gut told me that we, as a public, weren't being told everything. And my emphasis on the *gut* is significant: discernment can be accessed through the body. Truth is not always registered by the mind; most of the time, the body can give us clues to what is true and what isn't.

I had already been fascinated with conspiracy theories by then and had started to question the general societal narrative since my time in New York. My friends and I enjoyed reading and debating these theories while smoking pot, a drug that's known to expand your mind to different points of view. One of the theories we discussed revolved around the government's secret Area 51, and we wondered why it was so hidden. A friend whose dad worked for the government and had done some work at Area 51 said she believed it would be better that certain things be hidden from the public, because it would otherwise incite unnecessary fear for those who weren't ready to hear the truth.

At the time I agreed, but now, being more conscious, I don't agree, as I no longer automatically accept the stories I'm told. In the case of government secrets, I like to believe that people can handle the truth and that more fear is caused by being kept in the dark. It's almost like hiding a divorce from your children, even though they're aware that something is amiss. Or like hiding the truth from a little girl with leukemia.

And I understand now, from my own deep inner knowing and from the way my body signals to me, that other major tragedies in society are not necessarily what society tells us they are. I'm not denying that they happen. In elementary school, I clearly remember the clear-skied, sunny September day when my mom, who was usually at work, came to pick up my sister and me early, and on the walk home she explained to us what had happened with the twin towers in New York City.

In university, I was on lockdown after the Boston Marathon bombing, while authorities hunted down one of the suspects in the city where I lived. It was a frightening, dark time.

The darkness was real in all these tragic events, and lives were affected. What I question is the official narrative we are sold as a society. It would be naive to think that there aren't nefarious groups of individuals in the world who do not have our best interests in mind. My awakening broke whatever spell of misguided trust I'd had in systems, celebrities, government, and the media. In the case of the Las Vegas shooting, my awakening helped me see that not everything is as it seems on the surface. This awareness did not make me fearful; it just made me realize I had to look deeper at information that was presented to me.

Awakening, in other words, provides a foundation for critical thinking. Instead of looking outside for answers, I looked within. Awakening helps you discern which "truths" are actually true. It allows you to filter information through your own inner wisdom, as if your intuition served as your GPS back to the truth. This is about being sovereign, which is being your own authority.

Awakening isn't just about intuition, though; it also relies on the logical side of the brain and helps us match that to what feels right in our bodies. At the beginning of my awakening, I relied *too* much on my feelings and intuition, rejecting all news reports and even my own research. I even depended too much on conspiracies, which are also not provable. This was not conducive to being discerning, because feelings can be influenced by many different factors, and we need to have some source of legitimate data to confirm our intuition. Spiritual people are susceptible to accepting ideals at face value, if they're not careful, and if they don't develop an ability to discern. They can become too trusting and easily fall prey to false ideals.

The challenge is in finding the balance between external information and inner wisdom so that we can discover the truth that makes sense to us. But humans are innately intelligent, and we were also designed to be resilient. When everything looks like it's falling apart in the world, it's actually coming together.

I changed my relationship to the darkness in the world on my trip to Bali in the spring of 2018, around the same time I changed my diet and stopped wearing makeup. I was drawn to this place as a location of healing, self-discovery, and spirituality. Bali was all over Instagram as an idyllic travel destination for wellness-minded and entrepreneurial people. The island's rice paddies, palm trees, and acai smoothie bowls were impossible to ignore. But more than that, its energy drew me. Two of my current paths converged in Bali, a center for personal development and entrepreneurialism. I made a vision board, gluing on photos of palm trees and ornate temples, along with photos of Singapore, which was also showing up on Instagram at the time because of its infinity pool at the Marina Bay Sands Hotel.

Our family friend Kathy, from England, lived in Malaysia at the time because of her husband's job as a bursar at a private school there. This was the same friend whom I had visited in Norfolk when I lived in London. I thought it would be perfect to see her again because I was intrigued by Eastern philosophy since my awakening, and when I had seen her last, I had been in such a different place in my life. The plan was to visit her at her home and get scuba certified on Tioman Island, a small island off the eastern coast of Malaysia. Leading up to the trip, however, plans changed because of the scuba conditions, and she suggested we go to Bali instead. It seemed my vision board was coming to life!

I planned to go as a last vacation before officially launching my business later that spring, knowing I would not be traveling for the next few years. Just as I had been drawn to London and to New York, there was a reason I wanted to go to Bali. Similar to how humans have energy centers in their bodies, like the chakra system, the earth has different energy centers too. The chakra system consists of seven energy centers that run along the spine of the body and keep us balanced physically, mentally, and emotionally. Earth's powerful energy centers include Sedona in Arizona, Maui in Hawaii, the Bermuda Triangle, and Bali. I believe different places in the world activate different aspects of ourselves, so it's not random that we're drawn to specific spots.

I learned that Bali is a purification center for the earth's energy, although everyone experiences these energetic places differently, and some people, like myself, can be more sensitive than others. These locations tend to increase awareness of the energy or beliefs that are out of alignment with your true self so that you can face them, and then release them. This allows you to become more aligned with your authentic self. Bali especially helps with the cleansing and clearing of the energy of fear with regard to change. It was exactly where I was meant to be as I embarked on my entrepreneurial journey, with a lot of my emotional and spiritual baggage in tow.

The local people understand that Bali's energy can elicit awakening and transformation, and I found its transcendent energy to be unlike anywhere I'd ever been. I felt my nervous system fully present the moment we touched down on the tarmac. All my low-grade anxiety melted away. My senses opened up, allowing the pace of my breath to deepen and slow down. My heart rate slowed and evened itself as I took in the environment with wonder. The luscious green rice-paddy fields, spotted with blooming exotic flowers, which the Balinese wore behind their ears, took my breath away.

And so did the black-sand beaches, waterfalls, and sunsets. The kindness and generosity of the people were part of the healing experience too. They welcome you as if you are part of their own families. This was the first time I saw a society that integrates spirituality in their everyday traditions and culture, as they start the day with offerings of food, incense, and flowers to the universe. I noticed that they also tie black-and-white-checkered scarves around statues, trees, and parts of buildings, so I asked our van driver, Wayan, why these scarves were everywhere.

"They represent balance in Balinese tradition," he said. "Black symbolizes evil, and white represents good. Together they symbolize the coexistence of opposites and the ultimate goal of harmony."

To explain this concept further, Wayan pointed out the light and dark aspects of Bali at each of our stops around the island. One time, we saw a group of men on the side of the road gathered in a circle, and Wayan showed us that they were watching a cockfight.

"This is the dark side," he said.

To him, this was normal, and his matter-of-fact perspective gave me a much more realistic worldview—knowing that there is darkness present, instead of pretending it's not there; the important lesson is not letting it overtake your life's experience. The Balinese understand there will always be good and evil in the world and in everyone. They believe that there is no joy without sorrow, no night without day. In this way, they embrace these differences because they offer an opportunity to create harmony, growth, and balance. They coexist.

I had come to Bali to cleanse myself of darkness, but Wayan's lesson taught me that it's okay to have good and bad inside me and that these inner traits can exist in peace. I had come to the island feeling broken, still perceiving my career failures as unredeemable, even though more than two years had passed since I had left London. I was ready to go in a new direction and release the pain of the past, and Bali had that ability to heal and transform pain. It's no wonder it's such a draw to the rest of the world for this reason.

After visiting sacred springs and pools and being cleansed of negativity and pain with these healing waters, I felt renewed and forgiven. I no longer felt my past weighing on my being; instead, I sensed the tingle of excitement, of a fresh start. The darkness within me from my past had been blessed and seen with compassion. From the spirit of Bali and the deep healing it represents, I was reminded that I was a good person and that I deserved the chance to rewrite my life story. I have such fond memories of Bali because it was a light in the tunnel of darkness that had surrounded me for the past four years, since I'd first decided to head off to London.

Bali, in the company of my family friends, was a place of letting go, higher vibration, love, and healing. My friends, Kathy and her husband, Jim, had taken care of planning the entire trip and our activities, and I was grateful to visit the exquisite resort they stayed at, facing the beach on the westernmost tip of the island. Talking with Kathy about my entrepreneurial aspirations as we sunbathed was so helpful, because she'd had a successful business, a bustling local tea and cake café, back in England, which she had recently sold. I felt fully supported by someone who had successfully built a business around what they loved, something I didn't have yet back home. I had been to her shop when I visited her while living in London, and now it was as if I was coming full circle. I was grateful for her presence and the guidance she shared.

Life is a mix of the dark and the light, and that's what makes it beautiful. To know darkness is to know light. You, too, can find the balance between dark and light, but it doesn't require a trip to Bali. Stay close to the truth and keep your own channel clear. Keep a limit on how much you allow yourself to delve into conspiracy theories, or into the negativity in the world; if you're not in a clear state of mind, you will be negatively influenced by them. Go ahead and research topics you are curious about, and from there, make your own intuitive decisions about what to believe. It's good, and even absolutely necessary and healthy, to question our environment and surroundings in the same way I even questioned some of the practices in Bali. Just remember you are always the inner authority.

All of us at the Monkey Forest Ubud in Bali. My visit to Bali showed me that it was time to let go of the past and that I could be cleansed and forgiven for my mistakes.

CHAPTER 14

Rebirth

I can be changed by what happens to me. But
I refuse to be reduced by it.

—Maya Angelou

After I shed what was no longer serving me, I came face-to-face with old wounds and old stories about myself and what I was capable of in life. I had finally gotten rid of all substances that weren't contributing to my growth as a person. I was now experiencing life in a brand-new way, clearly confronting obstacles. I launched my business, Guide to Wholeness, in April of 2018 and started coaching people through the same process I had just gone through: clearing physical and emotional barriers to their health and wellness and aiding them along their paths to self-discovery, supported by the tools of essential oils. The name of the business came to me intuitively; I wasn't sure what to call it at first, so I asked my spirit guides to tell me. After a morning meditation, the name popped in my head so clearly, and I jumped up from bed to add it to my vision board right away. The coaching I was imparting to others was leading them back to their wholeness, showing them that they could be enough as they are and helping them let go of behaviors and beliefs that no longer resonated with them.

A spiritual awakening can be compared to the actual physical process of being birthed—being forced through a small space and feeling like you're out in the cold, away from the safety and security of the warmth of the womb, with paper-thin baby skin that hasn't fully formed yet. In the same way that birth trauma occurs, being rebirthed, or awakened, can also feel shocking.

When you're reborn, you may feel as if your worldview has completely flipped upside down and it no longer lines up with that of those around you. And once you no longer share that commonality, you may feel like, and be viewed as, an outsider. Your family and friends may not be able to understand why you've changed. Like, why you now prefer meditating or going on retreats rather than going out for brunch and to the bars. They may not understand why you stopped eating meat, or why you want to talk about the deeper meaning of life—or the afterlife. In short, you may feel like the odd one out for a bit. You could feel like you don't relate to anyone, or that no one understands you. You're starting all over again.

Once you're reborn, you will typically start to identify as *being* spiritual or developing a spiritualist ego. You might find yourself viewing people as either having a high or low vibration. You might think you have to dress in yoga pants and wear mala beads and make your home look like a spiritual sanctuary full of books, crystals, oracle decks, and meditation pillows. It's like when someone identifies as being vegan (trust me, I did that too) and then that becomes their entire personality. But this tendency is known as spiritual materialism, or spiritual narcissism, and unfortunately, once you identify with "being spiritual," you may be drawn to these types of people like a magnet in your rebirthing stage, just as I was. You might pity those who are still asleep, and you might even try to wake them up by recommending they listen to the spiritual podcasts or read the spiritual books that have changed your life, so they can also change and experience what you have. Yes, I was that annoying person too. I tried to change other people because that made me feel better about myself.

I felt like I *was* better than everyone else. I'd been able to transcend the matrix, and others who were still stuck in it just didn't get it. With my new-baby skin, all red and sensitive, I often felt personally attacked when someone even slightly questioned the new "me." So I built walls, using judgment as bricks, keeping myself safe and protected from those who were still complaining that their jobs sucked, still partying every weekend, and still getting frustrated about what they saw on the news every day. I was so "above" them that, naturally, I distanced myself. But then I felt deeply alone because I couldn't relate to those whom I once did.

Everything that was low vibrational and out of alignment in my life was coming up to the surface to be reviewed and released. This is a normal part of the rebirth process, and even if it feels as if your world is shattering, it's actually releasing what is no longer in alignment with your new way of being. Your old identity and ways of seeing the world, and your new purpose, are being rewritten. What you used to do to numb and avoid will probably no longer work. You may have to face false ideas and views of yourself, which you have held your whole life, through a new lens, and this new view will be reflected back to you head-on from your external world. You'll be going through an identity crisis of sorts, and there is a physical part of this experience, too, because you're an integrative being.

You might notice, for example, that you're craving random foods. For me, it was hash browns with avocado sliced on top. Or you might find that coffee (or any type of caffeine) will *over*stimulate you, now that your inner source of energy has awakened. You might see that your sleep patterns have been interrupted, and now you're waking up at three or four o'clock in the morning, because that is when the veil between the spirit world is thinnest and you can receive divine downloads and energy upgrades. Make sure to write down any messages you get when you do wake up at these odd hours; it's not by accident.

You may feel tingling, or extreme thirst, as your body integrates these energy upgrades and your soul comes online. You may notice you sweat profusely at night; this happens when your body detoxes old wounds and beliefs. I remember feeling alarmed at first, because these symptoms seemingly came out of the blue, but it's all part of the messy yet illuminating process of rebirth. Your body will go through changes similar to how newborns experience dramatic changes in their bodies during the weeks and months after they're born, except your changes will be on an energy level.

While everyone is unique in what sensations they may experience, the process of rebirth is universal. After things fall apart, like they did in my world, they slowly come back together in a brand-new way. And that's when you may find you are more compassionate and accepting of people the way they are. That's *true* spirituality.

Instead of focusing on everyone around you, you will begin to take more responsibility for yourself, and you'll come to realize that everyone is on their own path. You won't be as affected by other people's perceptions of you. You'll most likely feel more whole within and accept aspects of yourself that once seemed foreign and in flux. You'll likely stop being bitter about people not understanding you; you'll just learn to accept it. Your focus may turn inward versus outward.

Instead of trying to help others—or fix them—you'll most likely notice that you influence people indirectly by just being yourself, following your passions, and achieving your own goals. You don't need to tell them what to do because, when people see you living authentically, they'll see this is an option for them. Also, after a period of being alone, if that's your journey, you'll usually start to attract people into your life who do get you and who have a similar path in awakening and rebirth. You may learn to accept your family for who they are, and even if you can't talk about the same things with them that you once did, the love will still be there. One mantra from the book *A Course in Miracles*, which has no author but was "scribed" by Helen Schucman, helped me arrive at this place: "Only love is real." That's what spirituality is about.

You may go through multiple rebirths and awakenings in your life, some even in the same year, as you continue to commit to your healing. You may still get frustrated from time to time when you see other people asleep, and you may still feel the urge to help someone you feel needs saving. You may find yourself slipping back into your old ways now and then, as growth isn't linear, and then you'll go through the rebirth process again. But it won't be as disruptive as your first rebirth. So try to be thankful for the first existential experience of rebirth as one that paves the way for you to live a more free, expansive, loving, and balanced life.

CHAPTER 15

Spirit

Make your own Bible. Select and collect
all the words and sentences that in all your
readings have been to you like the blast of a
trumpet.

—Ralph Waldo Emerson

I was introduced, in my integrative coaching certification program in 2018, to the concept that different aspects of ourselves—physical, mental, emotional, and spiritual—are interconnected. Sometimes developing one area will fix another that was out of balance. For instance, developing your spiritual self can balance your mental self, allowing you to feel less anxious.

That was the case for me and, ultimately, for the clients I would work with. Seeking out a spiritual practice is not the first place many of us look to find relief from anxiety. But it was the only place left for me to look, after I'd healed every other system: the physical, the emotional, and the mental.

But what exactly is spirit? I didn't have a good model, while growing up, for what that meant. I knew I had a connection with nature; I felt safe and alive in it. As a child, I read books like Jean Craighead George's classic *My Side of the Mountain*, and I'd be inspired to "camp" in my yard until bedtime, foraging for my own "food" (just branches and leaves that I didn't actually eat). That part of me knew I was connected to something greater than myself.

But I lost sight of that part when I found myself in the largest metropolitan areas of the world. Although they were supposedly some of the most aspirational places to live, I felt more disconnected there from my true nature than I ever had before. Like a boomerang, I had to see the opposite of my true self—striving for status, chasing external validation, and living unhappily—to be shown the way back.

Spirit to me is an intelligent energy, and it had been a long time since I had accessed that part of myself, the part that just knew the truth without knowing how. As children, we are highly in touch with this aspect of ourselves, and slowly over time the systems in our society shut it down, bit by bit. It's why we remember our childhood with so much color and vibrance, when our vision of the world was brighter, as if the saturation were turned up. It's how children can make up entire worlds that feel lifelike to them.

Spirit is connected to intuition, which gives you the power to look within and find the answers. A higher version of yourself exists, and this aspect of you on a higher spiritual plane is always guiding you through life, even if you're not fully aware of it. Becoming aware can be especially helpful in making decisions that are in alignment. Intuition can't only be learned in a book. I discovered my intuition again after I'd tried following outer authorities such as therapists, psychologists, coaches, and business leaders—and getting nowhere.

I wasn't listening to myself, until I was forced to, when signs and themes began to show up more than once. I started listening to a voice that emerged within, an unwavering voice that would just say a word or two about what I was meant to do next. My commitment to my healing had allowed me to get to this point, to be connected with spirit in the present moment. This small yet mighty voice is what led me to start a business, to take a leap that I hadn't considered before.

I was only able to access this voice once I had slowed down. Once I had cleaned up what I was eating and putting into and onto my body. Once I was meditating. Once I did the work to delete the faulty programming in my mind. It's really hard to hear that still, steady, and sure voice within when you're on a hamster wheel or when you're dulling yourself with processed foods and toxic substances. The inner voice gets buried deep within.

Intuition is also a feminine quality. We currently are transitioning out of a masculine energy–dominant society, or patriarchy, which represents doing and achieving—constantly. Femininity represents receiving and stillness. No one quality is better than the other, and both qualities are found in men and women. But it makes sense that we can't hear our inner voices if we're constantly in action, because intuition is about *receiving* guidance. Fortunately, our society's emphasis on the masculine is changing, as we shift to a more equal, balanced, and whole society and embrace both the feminine and healthy masculine in all aspects: work culture, school systems, and more. Imagine being able to know things without needing anyone to teach you and, instead, being able to connect to and follow universal guidance!

I had never known there was a force like spirit that I could have complete faith in; I'd always thought I had to do everything on my own. I didn't know until I had gone through challenging times that I could call on archangels or guardian angels, or the universe, to support me halfway. Once I started down the personal development path, I also learned about the values of a compassionate self. Spirit is also known as the energy of love. To me, it's undeniable that a force as strong as love exists.

I learned from my awakening that *telling* the universe what I wanted (like ordering from a catalog) was an ego manifestation instead of a soul manifestation, which came from deep reflection within myself. Through my dark night of the soul, when I had to turn to a spiritual form of support, I realized this was a partnership, where I would cocreate life with the universe. This would result in favorable outcomes that were much more aligned with my soul, because spiritual wisdom comes from a higher intelligence than the limited mind of the human ego. Instead of manifesting things to feel better on the outside, soul manifestations bring us joy on the inside, from places where we wouldn't have looked before. This is true alignment with life, and the manifestation process is a lot more effortless because this is how we were designed to create.

You can receive guidance from the universe by noticing different signs and decoding their symbolism. Signs can show up in many different forms, and many can be personal and subjective. I view hawks flying overhead, rainbows, finding coins, feathers, and number sequences, like 11:11, as auspicious signs from spirit, confirming I'm on the right path. You may notice synchronicities, which are also messages from your intuition. I learned in a psychic development workshop that nothing is random. That's where synchronicities come in: the exact person that could help you appears at the right time, or you overhear a conversation that gives you the information you need. Notice in your life when there are synchronicities, also known as coincidences that can't be explained, and take those as clues to guide your steps in life.

For example, as I was writing this book, I was manifesting a dog into my life, based on a desire I had almost three years ago. I had the desire, but the timing was elusive. However, I noticed the synchronicities that showed me when it was possible to adopt a dog. My family friend got a black shih tzu puppy that was so adorable. Then my friend got a dog that she brought on a weekend trip we took to Vermont. A dog had seemed out of the realm of possibility for me because I didn't have one growing up, but spending time with my friend and her dog made it seem more possible. I continued to notice more coincidences: a colleague at work shared local resources for dogs and animal rescue shelters, and a neighbor told me all about how she adopted her dog from Puerto Rico. When I checked my inbox after meeting this neighbor, I found an email about a dog adoption event with dogs from Puerto Rico taking place that weekend. I knew I had to be there; it was all connected. Then a final sign confirmed that I was on the right path: I found a shiny penny on the sidewalk outside the adoption event, which signals confirmation for me. I knew I would find my dog that day.

Me and my little guy on his adoption day. It was clear from the moment I saw him that he would be my dog.

When you hear a song with a message that seems to provide guidance, you can also be receiving a sign from the universe. You may hear lyrics that motivate you. Or songs that comfort you when spirits visit or when you are trying to connect with your loved ones. My dad and I shared a favorite song: "Who Says You Can't Go Home" by Jon Bon Jovi. We listened to it in his red convertible, with the top down in the summer. Now, whenever I hear that song, I know it's my dad saying hello from the other side. Its lyrics had meaning that rang true for both of us, representing the life paths we each followed, traveling the world in search of something else and returning home again.

To me, evidence of spirit in action is the force that allows nature to function in synchronization, like how a butterfly emerges from the cocoon. Or how bees and flowers mutually benefit from the process of pollination. In a similar way, this divine blueprint is how your physical body's systems all work without you consciously having to think about your heart pumping to oxygenate your blood. It just functions. This realization that you are being supported by an intrinsic function can be incredibly comforting in those dark and confusing times when you are going through an awakening. It can help relieve anxiety that stems from not trusting that life is supporting you.

Developing a spiritual connection can help you navigate tumultuous transitions and bring you back into a state of love, presence, and feeling guided. Spirituality can mean something different to everyone. Some people may claim to not have a spiritual connection, but they find nature to be restorative and a source of inspiration. Yet what they may not realize is that having a connection to nature is one way of connecting to spirit. Early on my awakening journey, I explored different ways of connecting to spirit. I purchased a mala necklace to recite prayers on each bead, I read spiritual texts, I practiced meditation, I drank cacao in ceremony, I journaled, and I simply prayed. I used oracle cards, which taught me how to turn my challenges over to a higher source—my intuition—which would tell me to pick the right card with a message to guide me. My favorite deck was Crystal Angels by Doreen Virtue, and when you find a deck you connect with, it will be for a reason.

I learned to ask for support from spirit, from the universe, and that allowed me to trust in myself, knowing that it wasn't all on me, that I had far-reaching support. A spiritual practice is necessary to develop faith, a positive mindset, and resiliency as you develop career satisfaction, certainty, and self-trust. As challenges arise, your belief will act as your anchor to move through them.

CHAPTER 16

Boundaries

Daring to set boundaries is about having the courage to love ourselves, even when we risk disappointing others.

—Brené Brown

Boundaries, even if they seem upsetting at first, ultimately help set the tone for a relationship that is balanced for both individuals. Boundaries are meant to keep each person safe and heard, not to exile each other. But most people haven't been taught to set boundaries; instead, we are accustomed to our society's patriarchal structure in which, for women especially, there is a tendency to be submissive and not take up space. Setting boundaries for the first time *will* be jarring and often requires continuous reminders until the boundaries become clear.

When I went from being a complete doormat, catering to my family's expectations of me and my life rather than my own, to setting boundaries around how much time I would spend with my family, I was met with a lot of resistance and confusion. How could I be acting in this way, so different from who I had been until that point? I was guilt-tripped when I started pulling away and let my mom and sister know that I had to focus on myself and my business. I'm not sure they understood. Until 2017, I had been so enmeshed in my family that I didn't know who I was outside the relationship. When I came back home to Boston, I spent the majority of my time with my mom and sister and other lifelong family friends. It was part tradition, part expectation. Of course, I was grateful for these relationships, but I realized I allowed them to take away from my own individuality, my own social life, my own hobbies—from the person I was becoming.

Me, my mom, and my sister visiting family in France during my high school years. At that time, I didn't know who I was outside of this tight-knit relationship structure we had been in for so long.

I came to this realization after spending the Christmas holiday in 2018 at my mom's, with her partner, my grandma from France, and my sister. I hadn't been aware that we would be going to a church service with my grandma. At this point, I was clear that this type of faith wasn't for me; it was early in my awakening process, and this rigid type of worship wasn't an environment I felt comfortable in. I chose to not go to the church service with everyone else, which felt awkward when I stayed back alone. I had made waves in the family, and I realized after this weekend that I had to branch out. Later on, spending Christmas alone didn't feel so isolating. It felt freeing as I eventually realized I was stepping out of both family obligation and societal expectations.

Boundaries are meant to keep each person safe and heard, not to exile each other.

I had started to become aware of all the not-so-healthy family patterns at play in our interactions. For so long, I had allowed myself to be teased and poked at, but I was respecting myself now, and I wasn't accepting snarky quips anymore. I had zero tolerance for taking on the emotions of my family, and in fact, the wounds from my upbringing were being poked and prodded in our interactions. These wounds were triggering my hostility toward my family. When I would share what I was learning and what I was up to in my healing, or my business, I was aware that what I was saying sounded outlandish to them, and I felt judged. I was the black sheep of the family, the one unlike the others. I also was on shaky ground in my newfound sense of self.

After repeated efforts at setting limits around how many family get-togethers I would attend, which involved opting out of weekly family dinners and outings, I caught flack for not being there with everyone. There isn't one specific conversation I remember; it was mostly hearing that everyone wanted to see me and that it wasn't nice *not* to be there when everyone else was. A lot was happening on an energetic level for me (as an empath), because I had disrupted the pattern that had been operating beneath the surface: the pattern of holding on to everyone's emotional stuff for them. My voluntary departure from the family unit was bringing those feelings out in the open. They were all frustrated that I was focusing on my business more than on them, and they believed I was evading the family's unspoken rule of obligation. But I wasn't living my life fulfilling obligations to others anymore.

The only action that helped reset the relationship pattern and showed how I really meant business with my boundaries was going no contact. This wasn't easy for me to do, by any means. It's a heartbreaking decision that no one wants to make, and here I was doing it again, after I had done the same thing with my dad. Now it was with my mom and sister. I would have never imagined this happening, but sometimes it's necessary. The experience with my dad showed me that it was an option when the relationship was doing more harm than good for my mental health and development. I tried what I could, and at the end of the day, I couldn't control my family's behaviors or their healing timelines. Boundaries represented what I would and wouldn't endure in the relationships, and when they weren't respected, the situation snowballed and my sense of self eroded. I had to do what was best for me to move forward in my life and step out of unhealthy patterns that could have kept me stuck in an immature state. This split from loved ones is not uncommon when going through an awakening.

When I identified as someone who deserved to be walked all over, I was allowing this to happen. I look back to my early experiences working in London and New York, and even jobs after that, and I now see that a lot of the pain I experienced stemmed from the fact that I was a doormat, allowing myself to be stomped on. Boundaries represent choices, and had I set them back then, I would have taught others how I wanted to be treated. But setting boundaries had to start with my own clarity about what I needed in relationships and then communicating that to others.

I have identified with having a codependent wound, which is an underlying addiction similar to alcoholism, and I have deeply researched this pattern of behavior because it can show up in all areas of life. A person can be classified as codependent if they are psychologically manipulated by someone else who exhibits a pathological condition (such as alcoholism or drug addiction). The codependent wound is often perpetuated in TV shows and throughout our societal programming. For example, take the TV show *The O.C.*, which was my favorite while growing up and a cultural phenomenon of the 2000s. The main character, Ryan Atwood, falls in love with the neighbor next door, Marissa Cooper, in the affluent Newport Beach area. Marissa is clearly struggling with alcoholism, blacking out and getting into all sorts of trouble, and Ryan plays the role of caretaker, rescuing her in these situations and falling in love that way. It becomes clear, when we learn of Ryan's upbringing, that he played this same role for his mom, who was an alcoholic, and he was repeating this pattern in his love relationship. These were high schoolers playing out the typical codependent pattern of the rescued and the rescuer in addiction, and their behaviors served as a model love relationship for young teens to aspire to, whether they were consciously aware of that or not.

Codependency was perpetuated in my family's patterns when I was growing up. As my dad slipped deeper and deeper into alcoholism, my sister, my mom, and I grew closer as a way to protect ourselves and so we could lean on each other. But what worked in that situation served to harm us once my dad passed away because we were so entangled in each other's energy and not allowing ourselves to feel alone in the pain.

With my reading and research on the concept of codependency, I only understood it on an intellectual level, so I didn't know how to heal the emotions behind it. When I started learning about essential oils, I was curious and turned to my reference book *Essential Emotions*, which teaches how to use oils for emotional support. I wanted to see if there were any oils that might help. It turned out that tea tree, jasmine, thyme, oregano, and clove could all help heal codependency.

I started by diffusing these oils before bed in a water diffuser. I also made a roller blend with a few drops each of jasmine, clove, and tea tree, diluted with jojoba-seed oil, which I rubbed on my wrists throughout the day when I needed a boost. Over the weeks, I noticed that my need to please others, and my feelings of low self-worth, began to shift. Nothing else had changed in my routines, and I had to attribute this change to the plant medicine I was using. I started feeling more secure in myself and my body, and I felt more clarity about the boundaries between my energy and the energy emanating from others.

One of the most crucial lessons that empathic and highly sensitive people can master is owning what's theirs versus what belongs to others. It's all a matter of energy exchange, and by setting boundaries, you set the parameters for interpersonal exchanges. You can learn to set healthy boundaries. Boundaries give you the freedom to say no when you want to.

Codependency involves trying to control outcomes and perceptions so that you feel safe. Your view of yourself lies in the other that you give power to, because you are still reacting from that place where your inner child wants acceptance from parents and others for survival. And if our emotional, spiritual, and psychological safety was not taken care of adequately in our childhood, regardless of what our parents' intentions may have been, then as an adult we try to overcompensate for being out of control by being the one in control—but overly controlling.

CHAPTER 17

Mother Wound

The Mother Wound is the pain rooted in our relationship with our mothers that is passed down from generation to generation in patriarchal cultures and has a profound effect on our lives.

—Bethany Webster

One of the hardest things I had to do on my journey of self-actualization was to heal the relationship I had with my mom, and this included creating boundaries where I'd had none. I had to heal what is known as the "mother wound." I wasn't even *aware* that I had this wound until I had a shamanic healing in early November of 2018, where the healer showed me how my mom's energy was intertwined with mine and had been since I was three. My intention with this session was to retrieve bits of my soul, my consciousness, that I suspected had left my body when I was going through all those surgeries to fight leukemia. At this point, I was willing to do anything to feel more at peace, and I was open to this method of healing.

In my research, I learned that it's possible for parts of a soul to splinter off to avoid feeling tremendous pain during traumatic times, and this can happen even when one is in a coma. I had been in a medically induced coma for a week during my treatment, and now I wanted to call back the parts of me that had split off. While retrieving that aspect of myself was part of healing and accessing wholeness, another result was becoming aware of my mom's impact on me.

Growing up, I had a close relationship with her, which was special, but at the same time, it was very close. She had her opinions, which she shared with me, about whom I was friends with, what I could do with my body, and how I could spend my time. I wanted to feel free, but she parented in the only way she knew how, which felt slightly controlling. I exerted my independence more and more by the time I went to university, and later, when I didn't live with her anymore after university, I detached even more, bit by bit, without realizing it. I believe this was part of the underlying unconscious reason I wanted to move away so badly. I used to consult with my mom about all my life decisions, which is normal when growing up, but at a certain point, you become your own person and live your own life. By 2018, I was well aware of my father's impact on me, and I was on the path of healing the father wound. What I didn't realize was that my relationship with my mom equally influenced my development. It was just less obvious.

In the shamanic healing, I released a part of my mom's soul, with the support of the shaman, who extracted the pieces lodged in my liver and surrendered them back to my mom; the shaman did this all on the energetic plane. Only a few days later, I received a letter from my mom. It was out of the ordinary because I had been pulling away and I didn't normally get letters from her. In it, she expressed how she felt she had lost me and didn't feel the same connection we once had.

"It feels like a piece of myself is cut off and it hurts so much, and I love you very much," she wrote.

I was surprised to see the effects of the energy healing show up this way in the physical world, and her letter showed me how she realized the dynamic had changed on an energetic level.

I looked back to that time when I had been sick. My mom and dad took care of me by driving me to Dana-Farber in Boston a few times a week to receive chemotherapy, and on rare occasions, they slept overnight in the hospital when I needed to be there for weeks at a time.

Even at a young age, I was aware of the emotional and physical strain that my illness had on my parents. I internalized their sadness and stress. When I had the shamanic healing and we removed the part of my mom's soul, the shaman relayed to me that when I had been sick with leukemia, my mom may have never gotten over that grief. It stayed a part of her, likely because she didn't have the tools to cope at the time. Then, two years after the shamanic healing, I was in a session with my coach using EFT to heal my inner child. When the healer tapped on my meridian points, I became aware of something pivotal that had happened when I was young and developing my views of the world and of myself: I had developed an incorrect subconscious message that I was *indebted* to my mom for having leukemia and for all the emotional and financial stress that I had put her through.

It wasn't that I thought this consciously, or knew that my illness had hurt my mom, even if she might have mentioned it a few times. It was more that I knew and felt it on a subconscious level. Everything is energy.

As a child, even after I got better, I had this guilt for what I put my parents through, especially because it was no secret in our family that my dad never fully healed from that experience. My mom would mention that he didn't want to go to therapy for it. She said he had put that experience in a "little box, tucked it away in a drawer, never to be looked at again."

This guilt was like a debt that I hadn't paid off, and I tried over the years to pay it in different ways. I would attempt to please my mom, to support her emotionally and be there for her, as a way to pay her back. It was such a strong pull; I felt that if I didn't perform, make my mom happy, or put her needs above mine, then my own needs wouldn't be met. I pushed down any feelings of my own, like my anger toward her. The guilt was all I had room to feel.

I saw our relationship transactionally and had to give my half so that the bargain would be met. This not only played out in my relationship with my mom but also with my friends and work colleagues. I could only get my needs met, and feel seen and supported, if I was bending over backward first.

Your development as a person is significantly affected by the parent of the same sex, so my relationship with my mother had an impact on me, my other relationships, and my view of the world. I finally woke up to the fact that I was an adult, having made the transition from girl to woman, and I needed to make decisions in my life for myself, outside my family's input and influence. When I did, it seemed that my mom felt left out and unsure of the role she should play in my life. We had arrived at a transition point. I also got the sense that my mom was feeling confused about her role as "mom" in general, and her identity outside of that, because she was an "empty nester," now that both Lara and I had moved out on our own. Because raising us had been a major part of her life, she might have been missing that aspect. Even so, I couldn't allow the enmeshment to continue.

Most of us want to believe that all mothers deserve praise and unquestioned respect because they are the ones who gave us life. But a complicated bond is born from that belief, which leads to an unequal power balance. As a result, I hadn't learned how to show up fully as myself when I was with my mom, and in other relationships. I would always hold back, or mold myself in some way to gain her approval while subconsciously trying to not outshine her. It was as if there was some sort of unspoken agreement between us that I should serve her emotional needs in exchange for the parenting she had done. While I loved my mom and deeply appreciated everything she had done in mothering me, there were a lot of unhealthy aspects to our relationship.

It's uncommon to hear about this transition between mother and daughter as a young girl matures into an independent woman because of our societal programming around perfect harmony in mother-daughter relationships. However, it became an integral challenge in my own development. It still is, as I continue to be conscious of what I will and won't allow in our relationship, which is a dance that calls for balance as we navigate each new stage in our respective lives. To get to this point was difficult, and I did something I never would have imagined possible. The fallout that ensued showed how much of a shift I had made in our unhealthy codependent family dynamic.

After a few family gatherings where I realized how out of place I was feeling and how my newly emerging psychic abilities and everything I did were seen as foreign to everyone else, I realized I didn't want to be treated this way anymore. I had spent the last ten years of my life trying to exert more and more independence from my mom, yet I still felt she played too much of a role in how I made decisions. In society, we're shown how mothers and daughters can be best friends, and that's what happened initially between me and my mom. Without boundaries, I wound up telling her about everything going on in my life, but not every part of my life needed to be shared.

Although I cherished spending time with her, I realized it was taking away from my ability to make my own relationships and to build a relationship with myself. I wanted an adult relationship with her, so it was time for me to break off into my own adult self, not the daughter, or the friend. Relationships change and that's normal, which doesn't mean it doesn't hurt.

I could sense my mom pulling closer as she realized I was growing apart. I was going through my Saturn return, which is an astrological phenomenon that happens when the planet Saturn "returns" to the exact spot in the zodiac where it was when you were born. It takes about twenty-nine years for Saturn to complete a full orbit around the sun, so it's typically at this age to have your Saturn return. Its impact is felt into your early thirties. There's a second Saturn return that hits between ages fifty-seven and sixty, and I believe it's quite possible that my mom was going through her second return. This time is notorious for being a wake-up call to get your life in order. It teaches major life lessons on identity, and it illuminates when careers and relationships are out of sync. Saturn is a tough teacher that asks you to take responsibility for your life path and to honor your choices, even if they hurt another. It was a time of change in identity for both of us, and the greatest test to our relationship.

I let my mom know via text that I would need to take some time off from our relationship and that she wouldn't be hearing from me for a while. She didn't take it well and fought to at least continue phone contact with me. But I went through with my no-contact plan, even though it caused us both pain. She sent me gifts. She sent me letters. But I kept refusing them as invitations to connect. I threw them away. To heal codependency, refusing gifts is necessary because you are teaching the person that you cannot be swayed from your decision. Going no contact was going no contact.

I realized more and more that another person's actions are a reflection of their beliefs and view of the world, and I could only live my life the way I needed to. I knew how I felt about her, which was with deep love, but I was confused because I was not experiencing a healthy relationship with her. I was aware that I was hurting her emotionally, and it broke my heart. Still, it was the only way I saw that I could heal this relationship, and myself.

Without my mom in my life, I was in uncharted territory, but I felt I had some room now to become who I wanted to be. Our estrangement wouldn't be forever, but it would need to be long enough that I could gain some space to breathe and rebirth who I was really meant to be, the person whose worth wasn't tied to appeasing her mom. I could let go of the parts of me that wanted to take care of her, that wanted her approval so desperately, that wanted her counsel and insight on different aspects of my life.

The rift this caused in my family system actually served as a reset to a pattern that had been passed down through multiple generations. One thing I realized was that no-contact arrangements that are meant to be temporary fare best when there is a clear date for checking in with each other. In my situation, after six months of healing had gone by, I had forgiven her. But I was unsure how to reach out again because I didn't know what the new relationship would look like.

I was different; I had changed my mindset, my lifestyle, my friendships, my career, and my soul. One of the hardest parts of my reset involved learning to accept the fact that I would be misunderstood. It can be difficult to keep relationships after a separation like this, but it's not impossible. I had to navigate how the new version of me would be accepted by my family and friends. If they took issue with it, then that's when I needed to take a break. What I found was that once I was more accepting of my new self, the family was more accepting too. And then I became more accepting of them.

Everyone is entitled to boundaries, whether in relation to their work, intimate relationships, physical belongings, social media, family, food—you name it. You and only you will know what feels safe and healthy in your boundaries. I realized I needed distance from my mom in order to feel happy and like I had my own life. I had to learn that about myself, and then I had to teach her how I wanted to be in relationship with her.

Boundaries don't always need to be spoken; sometimes they can be gleaned by how you carry yourself and the energy you bring to the relationship. Know that, when you do set boundaries with someone, you are benefiting not only yourself but the other person as well. Anything you do for yourself in this way actually repairs any issues that this other person has had with boundaries too. You are teaching them a better way of living through your energetic example. By clearing up any unhealthy energy entanglements and setting ground rules for a relationship, you're influencing their higher selves in a positive way. You're showing them that they can claim their space by having boundaries in their lives too.

You may find, as I did, that setting boundaries and branching out to follow your own path sometimes leads to disapproval from the people around you. While they may be coming from a place of trying to save you from making decisions they don't think will serve you, this is not helpful to you. They're caught in the old perception of you, the old version of you. Although they may have known you for most of your life, they have only ever known one version of you. It can make them uncomfortable to see you change, especially if they don't know what to expect from you.

In my own life, when I decided to start a business, my family didn't think it was a smart idea, and I initially took it personally. We were an immigrant family, I was first generation, and the immigrant's mindset is rooted in creating security and following the typical career trajectory. Entrepreneurialism was risky and a threat to the family's security, at least their belief of it. When I took a pause on my relationships with family members, I was able to develop my own belief in myself and align with helpful people who were on the same path as me—or even a few steps ahead. This allowed me to be more understanding of myself and to be my own friend, for the first time. I eventually realized that my family's reaction was a reflection of how uncertain I had been, more than what they actually thought. I've learned to forgive them for their reactions, and I've also learned to do a lot of healing around people's choices that don't affect me personally. Keeping my business private has also been helpful in allowing me to come back into a relationship with my family. I'm not perfect at setting boundaries, by any means, but I always return to them.

Separation from family doesn't have to be a permanent thing, but in the early stages of awakening, when you're wobbly and finding your own footing, any negative influence can easily deter you from moving forward. It's like that newborn with new, thin skin—you're going to be more sensitive than ever before. You're most likely going to empathically pick up on the emotions of other people that may not be expressed with words. I learned how to better select the people in my life, by connecting with people who share similar values, who are on a path of developing themselves, who are respectful, and who are following their dreams. You will find your community and your sisterhood, too, but only after developing that belief in yourself, because it's hard for people to support you if you don't support yourself. Make sure to protect that belief in yourself by setting boundaries with anyone who's not on board with the "new" you.

Once, and if, you feel comfortable, you can allow your family of origin back into your life as long as you know that,

no matter what they say, you are able to handle it and maintain your belief in yourself. You can also choose to not engage
in talking about parts of your life that you feel will be judged
because of others' negative beliefs. As you experience this
transition with your family, you may also feel a disruption in
your friendships.

CHAPTER 18

New Friendships

We must be our own before we can be
another's.

—Ralph Waldo Emerson

I noticed the same splitting away with my lifelong friends too. I was changing, and we were growing up and apart. But it took a while for me to let go, and I felt like a real monster for doing so. These were friends who had been at my side for most of life, through all my milestones and in the tough times, too, like when I was let go from jobs and when my dad passed away. In society, we're not taught how to let go of friendships once we've outgrown them, and yet it's something that I want to talk about in order to normalize. Not all friendships are forever, and there's even a quote that says you have a friend for "a reason, a season, or a lifetime." The lifetime friend is rare, but I truly thought I had these friends because they had been with me for more than twenty years.

They were incredibly special to me, and ultimately, they taught me what it's like to have rewarding friendships and how to be a great friend. They taught me how to be a true listener—how to respect and be there for someone, to hold space for them, and to accept them for who they are. But even though I loved them and was grateful for their presence in my life, that didn't mean we were meant to remain friends forever. It's just like a romantic relationship: if it's not working, you don't stay in it just because you've invested so much time.

As I followed my dreams down an unknown path, I still maintained my university friendships, years past their expiration dates. It really was a case of *it's not you, it's me.* My friends were kind, supportive, caring, hilarious, and loving, but I was stepping into my new power when I wasn't with them and then acting like my old self again when I was with them. And that meant that when I was around my partying friends, I would most likely party.

Ultimately, my changing mindset, habits, and lifestyle led to a rift between them and me. This can happen when you're growing on different paths that lead in different directions. I had made up my mind to let them go, and then I began to doubt myself. *How could I do this? Was I doing the right thing?* I spent a long time contemplating it, and eventually I learned that you're meant to outgrow certain friendships.

Some naturally fade away, and others warrant a conversation. In most of these friendships, I felt we were moving on different paths and were naturally drifting apart anyway. The relationship with one of my lifelong friends was the hardest breakup of all, because it was a friendship that had started when I was one year old. Our mothers were friends, so we grew up together and had supported each other through elementary school to university, and beyond. We appeared in lots of home videos together, like the Halloween ones that showed how we had dressed up in matching costumes year after year. One year, we were both Mulan from Disney. We traveled together too; one year we went to visit my family in France, and I visited her grandparents' home in North Carolina another summer. I could walk through the front door of her house and make myself at home, and it was the same for her at my house. Even when we didn't chat or get together for months, we'd pick up right where we had left off.

I'll never forget how this friend, Anna, was there for me when my dad died. Even though she was back in Boston and I was in New York, we spent hours on the phone together the day he died, and she made sure I was okay before hanging up. She, and her family, helped us move my dad's belongings out of our old house and sell it for his estate. When I moved back to Boston from New York, she invited me to move into her apartment with her. I was in her wedding in 2019, and it was then, at that bacchanalian celebration, that I realized I was no longer on the same path in life as her. I loved her so dearly that it was confusing how much we had grown apart, but I knew that I just wasn't growing from our relationship anymore. I couldn't keep hanging on just because it was comfortable or because we had a long history. For a while, I simply didn't respond to her invitations to spend time together, but I knew I had to express myself more clearly. I needed to tell her that I didn't think I could be friends with her anymore.

I sent her a text in response to her request to spend time together. "I know I've been unavailable, and it's because I feel I'm pulling away and going on a different path. I've been thinking a lot lately about it, and I have to let our friendship go. Your friendship has meant so much to me and has made me the person I am today, I'm so grateful for it."

"There's a rainbow right now in the sky on our drive home," Anna texted back, "which feels beautiful as a way of signifying our friendship ending."

I still have love in my heart for her, and for all my past friends, for their pivotal roles in my life and for being part of my personal development. Their generosity, spirit, and trust throughout our times together have made my life meaningful. That never goes away. After spending much of 2018 and 2019 mostly on my own, I got clear about the type of new friends I wanted to call into my life. It took some time, but now my friends are powerful women who inspire me to be my most authentic self.

One of my best friends whom I've mentioned is Molly. She is a relationship coach and someone who has been on a deep healing path like mine over the past few years. She turned her healing into a successful business that helps others find romantic relationships. Since we met, she has connected me to a group of women entrepreneurs, where I have met new friends. Others in this group have become clients and collaborators in business.

From this group, Molly and two other women created a smaller women's group, which I was invited to join. We connect on topics about life outside of business. We now meet in this group once a month, virtually, and it's a space in which there's opportunity to share where we're at in life and what we would like support with. I feel seen and supported by these women—mostly because they have also committed to healing themselves, taking responsibility over their lives, and showing up for their dreams every day. This is not easy work, and it's not for the faint of heart, so I have much respect for people who do this, and I also tend to relate to them more than to other people not on this path. These connections have been medicine for me, allowing me to grow personally and professionally in ways that weren't possible when I was with my previous group of friends or even when I was on my own.

Some of my beautiful friends on a lake trip in the summer of 2021. After spending so much time feeling alone in transition and lacking a community, it feels even more rewarding to be in relationship with such powerful, sweet, and inspiring women. I did make friends who feel like sisters, who are working to be their best, and who are always down for a witchy ritual together.

There was an in-between period, when I didn't have many friends during this evolution, and that's normal. I tried to skip this stage and jump right into new relationships in order to leave the void behind. That caused me to choose people who weren't worthy of my trust or with whom I didn't truly resonate. I forced myself to try to establish relationships with people just to have someone to call a friend, willing to settle and take what I could.

For example, I had initially become friends with my first Reiki practitioner, Lauren, but it grew into an unhealthy relationship. There was a lot of competition, and it felt like she was jealous and wouldn't communicate her feelings. I had my own wounding around female relationships I was working through too. The boundaries between business and friendship were also blurred. While I cared for her deeply and this relationship taught me a lot, it made me realize how I need to be discerning when choosing my friendships, to ensure that people are working on themselves but also secure with themselves in the context of friendships.

I was especially susceptible to falling into unhealthy friendships and associations when I was raw from first awakening. That's something I wish I had been aware of at the time. Some things you just have to learn through experience. And there really is no way you can fail, because you'll always learn something in the process that you'll take with you in your next experience. Finding friends, I discovered, is like interviewing. You have to get to know someone first and build trust and intimacy slowly, before giving them the role of being your friend!

It's also important to judge people by their character a little more than by their lifestyle. For example, I tried to make friends with fellow vegans by going to a vegan spirituality Meetup group, and I realized that, even though we had veganism in common, we weren't a match on a personality level. Just because we had this one shared interest didn't mean we also shared one another's values. After going out for a vegan dinner together, I learned how these people liked to party with drinking; therefore, they were not my cup of tea. I *do* think it's important to align with people who understand and view the world in the same way as you, but it's equally important to know people who view the world differently. Both are important.

It will feel validating for you to know people who can support you on your journey and vice versa, but you'll also be a much more understanding and compassionate person if you can hold other viewpoints without judging. Especially in the world we live in now, being able to hold opposing viewpoints is more important than ever. Just know that it's okay to stand on your own for a while.

It's also important to judge people by their character a little more than by their lifestyle.

Now I set my intention to find the people I need in my life in response to whatever answers I'm seeking at the time, and I intuitively check in with myself to see whom I should turn to if I don't get the answers on my own at first. Intention setting is half the work it takes to create change in your life. This means clarifying the outcome you desire, and this clarity is what allows you to direct your energy toward creating this change. I used to struggle with asking for support—and sometimes still do—but my friends now are there for me. That's because I set the intention to be aligned with people who are for my highest good, and I allowed the universe to bring those people into my life. It's so vulnerable asking for help, but I've learned I deserve it, just like the love and support I give to others. In letting go of the identity that I'm the "strong one" and don't need connection and love from others, I've recognized my emotional needs.

Intention setting is half the work it takes to create change in your life.

I used to get so caught up in my relationships that I would lose myself in the process. This is why it was so disconcerting when I moved to London and was alone for the first time. It was like I only knew myself in relation to how others perceived me. It was a way of avoiding myself, because I could distract myself by spending time with others. Until my dad passed away—that's the first time I turned inward and got to know myself by taking the time to grieve and pause my excessive social life, which had been getting in the way of my goals, both personally and professionally. I had been more concerned with being accepted, spending time with others, and having a good time than with moving forward and getting clear on what it was I wanted in life.

Friendships can easily act as subtle distractions; if you're not careful, you lose yourself in them. But if you are solid in your sense of self, friends will offer you clarity when you're confused, strength when you feel weak, and a soft cushion of love when you're lonely or blue. Now that I have healthier friendships, I have the space to get clear on what I want to do next in my business, or with my creativity, without getting entangled in other energies. And as it turned out, I'm grateful for that transition time in between my old group of friends and my new ones because it solidified my ability to become my own friend first.

My mom and I spent a lot of time on the beach together in the summer of 2020, which makes sense because the beach is a healing and cleansing space. My own healing and my new understanding of mother figures freed me to be in a healthy relationship with my mom after our struggles.

CHAPTER 19

Self-Worth

No one saves us but ourselves. No one can
and no one may. We ourselves must walk the
path.

—Buddha

Being lonely can help you learn to rebuild your self-worth based on *your* approval only, but it's uncomfortable when you've always sought that approval from others. It can feel so foreign to have to give it to yourself. For the better part of 2018 and 2019, I was expanding my meditation practice, changing to a plant-based diet, and developing my career and business. But I was also living in that uncomfortable in-between period of relying on myself.

My social calendar used to be filled with dinners, brunches, nights out, and group travel. To go from that to just one or two friends to no one was a transition that came along with changing myself internally. But once I started to see my own self-worth, I was able to make better choices because I was living without the influence of others. I wasn't concerned with what my peers would think, because I would no longer be seeking their approval, whether that was a conscious choice or not.

Initially, I felt self-conscious as I wrote this book, because, in the back of my mind, I had a little annoying voice (my ego) saying I don't write well enough or my writing isn't engaging enough. Even though I've worked on my self-worth through meditation, affirmations, therapy, and coaches, self-validation will be something I continue to work on throughout my life because of how I was programmed while growing up. As a woman in a patriarchal society, you're subconsciously taught that your value is less than that of a man's. You're taught that your role is to serve men, look good for them, be chosen by them. That's what the Disney princesses—like the one in my childhood-favorite movie, *Sleeping Beauty*—demonstrated: wait for a man to save you from your eternal sleeping spell.

Our entire society, though, is programmed to feel not worthy enough. It's how we are marketed to constantly, especially as women. Makeup, hair products, clothing, and dieting are pushed on women with the message, *You're not enough as you are. You need these items to look and feel you are enough.* If we felt worthy, we wouldn't see the need for these products. That's what companies think, which means they profit off our insecurities. That's what it's like living in a materialistic and capitalistic society.

I used to adore reading magazines when I was younger. I would accompany my dad to do the grocery shopping so that I could sit down in the aisle and go through all the teen magazine articles about celebrities and how to dress like them and do your hair and makeup like them. And how to lose weight like them.

This programming makes us learn to view people for their outer physical traits and to value ourselves only with respect to our physical traits. It's a common theme I see with my clients too: a feeling of not being enough or not feeling worthy of what they want, like a satisfying career or a life that lights them up. I know this is a universal theme of suffering, because it's so pervasive in our society.

This is a crucial wound to heal, because it touches so many areas of your life: your career, your finances, your relationships. We settle for less in our careers because we conclude that we don't deserve more. We don't negotiate our salaries or express when a boundary has been crossed in a working relationship because we don't feel we have the right to.

Everything is energy, and the energy we put out tells others, and the universe, how to treat us. When we learn to heal from the patterns we developed while growing up, and from traumatic events we've had to face, we can rewrite our perceptions of self, and our self-worth then grows automatically. Self-worth also grows when you choose yourself over and over and when you acknowledge that you are loved by a higher power. You can do this by acknowledging the small wins and, on a larger scale, by recognizing when you made it through a challenge, somehow, even if it seemed impossible at the time. It's not possible to fall backward and regress on your personal development path, by the way. The fear that your patterns will resurface and haunt you isn't real unless you give meaning to this belief. Even though we sometimes feel as though we're spiraling backward during the healing process, to a place in our past, we are really moving forward.

One of my clients, Mary, was looking for a new job after being laid off from a company. We had met a while back in a career-networking group, when she was looking for the job that she later got laid off from. She came to me after this latest setback. She said she saw how I had managed to come back from setbacks and find a career and business that I love, which, more importantly, gave me a lifestyle of travel and financial freedom. For that reason, she wanted to work together, since she knew it was possible to land somewhere perfect for her.

The main issue Mary had was in understanding how this repetitive cycle of getting laid off was telling her something about herself. We tackled this right at the start of working together, because if this underlying belief about her not being able to stay at a company for a long time didn't change, she'd keep repeating the cycle. Also, based on my belief that everything happens for a reason, we looked at how the roles she had taken since university had been wrong for her. Did she really feel challenged by what she was doing? Did her jobs use her skills and interests? Did she work with people she liked? I invited her to consider the idea that perhaps these jobs didn't work out for a reason—because they weren't right for her.

We dove into many career options together, which may have looked messy on the outside when looking in, but it was all part of the process. I had done the same thing when I was looking for my ideal career and when I started my business. I had explored all the options that piqued my interest, including graphic design, Fulfillment by Amazon selling (yikes), and even retail.

Mary was intrigued by videos made for commercial real estate marketing, so we looked into video marketing. She was also inspired by architecture, so we looked at that as an area of marketing she could work in. She knew she didn't want to be stuck behind a computer all day, and she wanted to connect with a team. She was really a people person, and her previous finance roles had not offered this key element of fulfillment to her.

Sometimes it takes exploring every angle to know that you're not missing a better option. Doing so can help you identify the most important elements you'd like to have in your role or business, and it can also inspire future projects for which the timing might not be right yet but will be at some point in the future. Mary and I first focused on what was within her control, and she wanted to make sure she chose a company with foreseeable longevity.

Second, we focused on what was beyond her control. It was out of her control that the start-up she had previously worked for was sold. She could frame this circumstance as outside her control in job interviews, now that she was clear on what was and wasn't right for her.

An accomplished woman, Mary was accustomed to reaching her goals, but she had become dejected by these recent setbacks. I knew that feeling because I had been there too. It took a lot longer for me, *four years even*, to really believe that I was not my failures and that they in fact had led me to greater success. One of the ways that I've been able to move through this has been by investing in coaches to guide me, using their acquired wisdom to light the way forward for me.

Having experienced this sense of failure, I was able to help Mary own her perception of herself, which in turn would help her teach others how to treat her too. If she believed she was a walking mess that brought failure no matter what she did (victim mindset), then others would believe this too. What she needed to do was gain clarity about this new perception of herself and what her intention was for her career, and then she would be ready to talk with the right people in her network, who could then connect her with the right opportunity. Mindset is behind action, and that is why rewriting your story is at the core of the work that I do with clients.

The story I needed to rewrite for myself during my healing process was that I was worthy of love, which meant I needed to start with loving myself. I needed to feel a deep certainty and grounded self-assurance in myself that was stronger than my old way of being had been, when I'd believed that you could "fake it till you make it." I needed to develop a self-love that was as genuine and natural as breathing, where I didn't need to pretend. That way, there would no longer be a gap between the confident persona I played on the outside and the scared little girl I felt on the inside. Those negative beliefs were not true, and when I let them go, and replaced them with positive views and a growth mindset, I was free to experience true joy and self-love.

In being aware of the role I played in every one of my life challenges, and the role others played, I was able to take ownership of my narrative. I could pinpoint exactly when I had grown from the challenge and what I had learned for the future. I'm no longer at the whim of others' perceptions and judgments, or even my own self-judgment, because I've examined when I played a role and when I didn't, and I've forgiven myself for the poor choices I made, because I was acting with my best knowledge and doing the best I could at the time.

Self-respect and acceptance have touched every area of my life: my financial abundance, the integrity of my relationships, and my career opportunities. I have a lot more control over how I could show up than I thought I did. When I realized how much value I provided, not only in my guidance for others but also in my digital marketing skills, I started to charge a higher price for my work. I learned how to negotiate and sell myself, with the idea that this would help me help more people.

And once I saw how valuable I was, I was in a position to teach others to see me that way too. When your whole perception of yourself changes, your whole outer world changes too. If you can own your story, you can influence others' perceptions. It starts from within, and it doesn't all happen overnight. It took a period of over three years for me, and even though in the beginning I wanted to hit the fast-forward button (sometimes I still do, but patience has been one of my greatest lessons), I learned to be grateful and content with myself in the moment. That's how I can get my clients there in a fraction of that time, by imparting guidance from my experiences, without having them spinning in circles, repeating their same behaviors. This defeating situation, when stretched out over years, can lead to dwindling stores of faith and self-worth, and that's why coaching is so valuable.

My changing self-perception led me to write this book. Even with this new project, I've had to make myself focus on the redeeming aspects in order to overcome the challenges along the way and keep momentum. I would need to put in my own effort, and although others could provide some guidance, no one was going to do the work for me. It would take trial and error, self-love, and dedicated time and effort in the same way that all those factors helped me discover what an authentic life looked like for me overall. Before discovering my own self-worth, I found myself trying desperately to align with clients, team members, and mentors—some of whom weren't a good match for me. I gave my power away, both to friends and to coaches. I especially let coaches take the wheel of my life. I didn't know any better back then, and I now look back at myself, during that period, with loving affection as if I were watching a toddler learn how to walk.

Trial and error is messy, and many people don't like to have to make mistakes in order to find what works. It takes humility to be willing to fail in order to succeed, and this approach is necessary for a career transition and life in general. As a former perfectionist, who had followed all the steps laid out by society to be successful, it was truly terrifying to deviate from the plan and become the captain of my own ship. In 2018, when it felt like I was walking in a forest with no clear path to my destination, I started to learn to trust that I was being guided by spirit, by my dad, and by my ancestors. I learned I wasn't meant to do it all alone, and when I discovered I was receiving support from unseen spirits, all conspiring for me to succeed, I was able to view myself in a different light. I could no longer feel unworthy if I had others reflecting back to me that I was enough as I was. That's when I also started to learn that I could trust myself to make the best decisions for my life rather than outsourcing that responsibility to others, as I'd done until then.

Building a relationship with intuition takes time, and it takes practice, like building a muscle. Once I believed that everything was happening *for* me, not *to* me, I was able to build my self-trust and faith in the universe. Believing that everything happens for a reason, that nothing is random, and that what's meant for me will never miss me, allowed me to let go of that old anxiety that always expected doom.

CHAPTER 20

Self-Knowledge

Knowing yourself is the beginning of all
wisdom.

—Aristotle

Now when I tell people my story, they can't believe that I am
the same person I describe in those earlier years. And, truth-
fully, I'm not. My experiences showed me what I do and don't
want for myself. Often, we're prompted to learn more about
what we want by coming face-to-face with the experiences that
show us what we *don't* want.

In 2019, after my awakening and a year after I started
my business, I made the decision to go back to working full-
time at another company. This had not been my initial plan;
I'd thought I would work full-time in my own business. I had
learned what I didn't want in a role and a company, in challenging circumstances. What helped me make this decision to
return to full-time work was the realization that my energy
worked best when my income wasn't centralized on one point.

I also realized I was living with the notion that I had to be one thing: just an entrepreneur or just a full-time employee. By then, I had exposed myself to enough roles that I realized how being just an entrepreneur wasn't going to honor my complete identity.

So, I went where I was needed. I asked the universe to use me in the best way to serve the highest good for people. I had already been helping local businesses and family friends with their marketing since 2017, which helped me learn how other entrepreneurs managed and marketed their businesses. Later, I began to learn how to market my own business successfully, and I further developed this new set of skills. Throughout those years, I also discovered that my skills and experience are appreciated and that, in the right place with the right mindset, I could thrive.

I have found that learning about myself required many approaches and assessments, including Human Design, My Genius Test, and astrology charts. I wrote about these tools in my most popular article on Medium, "How to Choose a Career That Fulfills You—While Keeping Your 9–5," for the Better Humans publication.[1] These tools helped me appreciate myself and look at my "weaknesses" as my strengths too. They showed me that, although I'm not perfect, I don't need to be in order to feel worthy.

Human Design is one of my favorite comprehensive tools. It combines astrology, the I Ching, the chakra system, and kabbalah in a system that was channeled by Ra Uru Hu. This system recommends ways to manage your energy based on your type and profile number, which you find by inputting your birth date, birthplace, and birth time. Once I found out I

---

1. Emily Smith, "How to Choose a Career That Fulfills You—While Keeping Your 9–5," November 13, 2020, Medium, https://betterhumans.pub /how-to-choose-a-career-that-fulfills-you-while-keeping-your-9-5 -47462bbf6569.

was a Reflector, matching roughly 1 percent of the population, I learned that I operate differently from the other four types (Manifestor, Manifesting Generator, Projector, and Generator). This tool completely changed everything about how I manage my energy and my work. It honestly changed how I live my life, because it suddenly showed me the reason why I felt like such an alien in all my environments, turning into a chameleon trying to fit in. It also gave me insight into how I needed a slower pace, and more time to make my decisions. In other words, fast-paced careers were not right for me. And it taught me that I work best in a team, not fully on my own as a solo entrepreneur, because I'm what's known as a non-energy being in Human Design. My chart looks all blank, when it's typical to have the chakra centers filled in with colors for the other types. A non-energy being thrives when they can "reflect" other people's energies as their own.

You can find out your type by running your chart on myBodyGraph (mybodygraph.com). I highly recommend listening to my podcast episode "How to Live Intuitively Using Human Design" (find it at www.guidetowholeness.com/podcast). It goes deeper into how Human Design works with HD teacher Kezia Kraus, whose husband helped to develop the myBody-Graph website.

My Genius Test, another assessment tool, classifies personalities as four genius types. This system pulls in imagery from the four seasons and four frequencies found in ancient Chinese and Indian thought (similar to traits that Aristotle and Plato identified too). You can find this test on GeniusU (app.geniusu.com/my-genius-test).

High-performing teams work best with a variety of personality types. Once I found out I was a Blaze genius, representing the fire element, I realized that my genius is in working with people. I needed a role where I could connect with lots of people, making a difference. Neither working remote, as I had been doing during the COVID-19 pandemic, nor working on my own were good fits for my disposition. I also needed fun and variety, work that wasn't number focused, and leadership through communication.

Now I have all my clients use these tools to learn how they can draw on their strengths and be aware of any weaknesses. I've seen how having this awareness of themselves has led my clients to choosing career paths that bring them purpose, connection, and financial abundance.

If you're a fan of more esoteric insights, learn what your life path number is. This gives you insight into your life purpose. I'm a life path seven, which means I'm a seeker. I'm always reading and researching, and I like roles where this is built into my job description.

Personality tests offer ways to think about what makes you unique—whether or not you believe their underlying premise or even the results. What these tests all do is give you a starting point to consider your inherent personality traits, preferences, and the purpose you serve for humanity, from an objective standpoint.

The reason I take my clients through all this—and why I wrote this popular article on Medium about finding work that fulfills you—is because I was only able to find a full-time role that I truly enjoy and that aligns with my gifts and values by knowing myself through committing to this inner work. All the previous experiences along my career path had showed me what I enjoyed and what I didn't. I had been in too many jobs that weren't right (perhaps you can relate), which caused interpersonal issues and lack of performance and growth. All of this was due to a lack of research and introspection before job hunting. I've learned that it doesn't benefit anyone to choose a career that's not rewarding to you.

Finding a career that you truly enjoy, feel inspired by, and can be paid well for is completely possible. I am grateful to have found fulfillment as a digital marketing and brand manager at a female-founded company that supports employee health and safety initiatives in the life-science industry. My role combines all the best aspects of the careers I had tried on in the past. A big part of my day-to-day role involves branding, by creating social media designs with Canva and basic Adobe, which satisfied my love for graphic design without making it everything I do.

I write all the social media captions, email campaigns, and website updates, and sometimes I blog for the company. This satisfies my love for writing and my need for variety. Part of my role also supports employer branding, which gets me into contact with all the employees in the company, making the most use of my Blaze genius. I've learned a thing or two about what type of culture attracts the right people, by learning what makes up a culture in my varied experiences. A company that I want to work for has clear values, pathways for growth, and leadership that is actively listening to employees.

I get equal amounts of time connecting with others and working introspectively on content, and I realize I would be missing that if I only worked on marketing. I also don't work on client management anymore, which is what I decided was not for me from previous roles. But when I do need to interact with clients, I feel more comfortable doing so.

I chose a company that has been around for almost thirty years, after the negative experience of working at a start-up operation in London that wasn't off the ground yet, offered insufficient structure, and was burdened with too much overlap in role responsibilities. But I did learn there that I preferred working in a smaller company, where I'd have more flexibility to make an impact. Since I chose to work in a smaller company's internal marketing department, I get to wear a lot of hats and see the effect that I'm making right away, which I missed when I worked in a large corporation. I also feel emotionally aligned with the mission of the company, which supports safety for scientists who are creating cures for diseases and cancers.

I spent years trying to get to a place where I loved my career, without any formal process. I spent most of that time just daydreaming of a career I was passionate about, and I took whichever freelance jobs I liked in any given moment. It took me eight months completely dedicated to this discovery process and job searching to land my role. Because of my experience, I'm now able to help my clients do this in half the time. But no matter how long it takes, the process is entirely worth it. In many cases, the longer the wait, the greater the reward.

The more I learned about who I was, instilling new belief and respect in myself, the better I was able to establish a life outside work that reflected this and to let go of the distorted mindset that my career was my identity. I now set the intention to expand my identity outside work by pursuing hobbies, participating in spiritual rituals, developing fulfilling relationships, and creating my own art. Altogether, these various aspects of my life show me that I'm multifaceted.

Think about it: usually a problem prompts you to make a positive change in order to rectify that problem. No matter how healed or successful you are, there is always a next level that you can reach. I've heard this from highly successful people in the personal development space and in my sphere: they still experience old patterns of anxiety and burnout from over-identifying with work, people, or even place.

Old patterns, such as boundary issues, don't necessarily go away entirely. They can still pop up, especially during times of stress. I believe this can happen any time we're not fully present and aware, because that's when our old stories, childhood trauma, and limiting beliefs resurface.

This doesn't mean we'll be plagued by these issues for the rest of our lives—quite the opposite. What's happening each time a pattern comes out to play is that the universe is giving us an opportunity to heal it further. It's like a release of energy from that pattern of thought, brought into our awareness, to help us chart a new course of action, by responding differently this time. That course of action can lead us to change. Managing these patterns is like pulling weeds: we pull them out when we notice them, thereby removing their ability to negatively affect us. It's key to remember to accept ourselves throughout this process, including our pasts, our old beliefs, and even many of those choices we made back when we were in survival mode. This is part of knowing yourself fully, and it's something you may have to continually remind yourself of. When I was growing up at home and it didn't feel either physically, spiritually, or emotionally safe, I had to behave in certain ways to survive. Now I have to accept this part of myself.

This need to remind myself of acceptance showed up later in life, in my twenties, when I would conceal parts of myself, including my spiritual interests, so that I'd be more accepted by others. This was codependency at its finest. Codependency and trauma go hand in hand, and trauma is something I've learned we all go through on varying levels, individually and collectively. In a course I took on ancestral trauma, the premise was that we are traumatized as a society; some people are more traumatized than others, but on some level, we have collectively experienced trauma. We also carry generational trauma in our cells. This is why we might have picked up limiting mindsets around money and resources, if we had grandparents that grew up in the Great Depression, for example.

Spending more time alone once I arrived home in Boston, going on retreats, and meditating allowed me to learn more about myself and what my preferences are. Each day is part of the foundation for the rest of our lives, but it does not need to define the course of our lives. We are entitled and able to heal and transform from our challenges and wounds as we get to know ourselves better.

CHAPTER 21

Creativity Heals

I found I could say things with color and
shapes that I couldn't say any other way—
things I had no words for.

—Georgia O'Keeffe

*Me coloring in bed when I had chicken pox. I loved this pink lap desk since it let me
color in comfort.*

I've used art as therapy and as a way to express my emotions since I was a little girl. When I was in the hospital, an art therapist came by my room and asked me to draw or paint how I saw myself. My mom told me the story of how I drew myself to look like Thumbelina, a Disney movie character whom I loved watching at that age. I saw myself as a little fairylike creature hiding in a flower, vulnerable, and taking on the world on my own. This was an eye-opening exercise that allowed me to get my emotions out onto paper, and I remember wishing the therapist would come by my room more often than just once every few weeks. But we also had a play area at the hospital, with plenty of art supplies to make creations, when she wasn't around, and my favorite art supplies were the sparkling glitter and paint.

In middle school, I went to weekly oil-painting classes, where I'd paint landscapes patiently over months at a time with a group of other kids from my school. I remember loving the conversations we'd all have about painting and art techniques, and I also recall feeling so at peace. When the course ended, I framed my rendition of a Monet piece with poppies in a gold ornate frame, feeling so proud of what I had created.

Other than photography class in high school, I went for almost ten years without a creative hobby or passion. In 2018, I realized I needed to reconnect with my creativity. By then I hadn't been drinking for two years, and I had just cut out my last crutch, marijuana. It was time to find something better to do with my time, so I threw myself back into painting. I bought canvases and acrylics at Michaels and started becoming familiar again with color blending and painting my favorite sceneries, like sunsets and the beach. My creativity came back online, and I noticed how expressing myself in this way helped me feel more confident in my work and life as a whole. Once I took that first step, the universe showed up and connected me with a colleague who had a spiritual art studio, called Creative Spirit, in Marblehead, Massachusetts.

During the shamanic soul-retrieval healing—where I had reintegrated the pieces of my soul that had splintered off to avoid trauma and released the part of my mom's soul back to her—I realized I had a connection to the moon. In that session, the shaman, Miriam, had seen a moon lighting up the dark sky, representing the darkness I was experiencing at that point in my healing journey. She referred to the moon as Grandmother Moon and helped me see how the moon is always there, in my darkest moments, acting as a beacon of light, of support. Later, after learning that I am a Reflector type in Human Design, I saw how I make major life decisions by waiting a full lunar cycle. Since the moon was a guiding light in my life, I decided to paint a piece with the moon going through its phases. I submitted this piece to the art studio and was thrilled to exhibit it in a show called *Shadow.* It was perfect timing because I was going through a healing of my own shadow, through a course on shadow work and my own journaling and reflection.

I was going through the dark night of the soul in awakening, after my world had shattered, and it had felt as if years were going by with no end in sight. It was an in-between period when my old ego—my old self—had died, but I had no idea what to do next in my life.

Gallery Exhibit

Shadow

Sept. 29 - Nov. 18, 2018

Wine Reception: Sat. Sept. 29, 6-8pm

CREATIVE
SPIRIT

Artists:
Kathryn Bartholomew,
Lynn Bradovchak, Josie
Bray, Michelle Brown,
Maureen Cotton,
Jacqueline
DeNisco, Rob Festa, Amy
Gray, Margaret Herrick,
June Jordan, Emily
Kwong, Karen Matthews,
Ginny O'Brien, Ron
Pruett, Emily Smith,
Melissa Tavares,
Nicole Werth

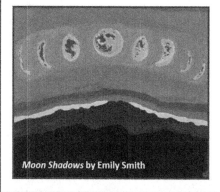

Moon Shadows by Emily Smith

Creative Spirit, *center for creativity & personal transformation*
www.creativespiritma.com | 781-797-0389
80 Washington Street | Marblehead, MA

My painting Moon Shadows *was displayed at my first exhibit. To me, the painting symbolizes making beauty out of my darkness.*

"The more you heal," my friend Molly says, "the more your creativity can come through." I committed to my healing when I realized it is for a greater purpose than just me. Also, creativity and healing work synergistically: the more you express creatively, the more you heal. Writing has become a calming and clearing practice that allows me to make sense of my emotions and organize them; if a few days go by and I don't write, I feel sick and imbalanced.

I knew when I committed to writing this book that I would be coming face-to-face with my past and the parts of myself I've kept hidden from the world. Healing and creativity remove emotional blocks and allow you to share the full spectrum of your beautiful being to the world. Whether it's through dancing, coloring, writing, photography, or sewing, there are so many fun ways to express your soul. I recommend *The Artist's Way*, by Julia Cameron, to my clients, and funnily enough, I found it when I was in the first stages of writing this book.

I had been at Barnes & Noble picking up books like *On Writing* by Stephen King and *On Writing Well* by William Zinsser when the red lettering on the cover of *The Artist's Way* caught my eye. This book, which the universe put on my path at just the right time, taught me how to access my subconscious through writing daily morning pages. By getting all my thoughts out on paper, I could write better. The book also showed me the innate spiritual aspect of writing, and how you can connect to another realm through creativity.

Once you access your innate creative nature, you'll find that other areas of your life flow more easily too. So many people believe that they aren't creative, after going through societal programming that doesn't value creativity. But they are wrong; we each have a right and a left side of our brain. No one is exempt from that. How you choose to use your creativity is up to you.

CHAPTER 22

Breathwork

There is one way of breathing that is shameful
and constricted. Then, there's another way:
a breath of love that takes you all the way to
infinity.

—Rumi

Breathwork is one of the most effective tools for pulling up
stuck emotions in the body that stem from past experiences. It
can also be the most empowering, as you're able to heal yourself with your own breath. A powerful experiential tool and
process that draws on ancient healing and spiritual practices,
breathwork allows deep self-exploration, transformation, and
healing at all levels of self.

The breathwork practice that I'm trained in uses the power
of breath, your body, intuitive cues, and music to help you
access an altered state of consciousness. It is not meant to be
relaxing; those effects come after the practice. I use a three-
part process, which involves inhaling and exhaling through

the mouth and uses the breath to act as a scrub brush to clear stuck emotions in the heart and stomach space. This helps to then balance the nervous system and allow emotional expression more fully than through simply talking. Breathwork helps you trust and feel safe in your body; clear the toxic cocktail of past experiences, wounds, and trauma; and reinvigorate a connection to intuition.

I initially resisted breathwork as an emotional regulation tool when I first experienced it in a virtual group event in 2018, because it was not easy. But just like the rest of my healing journey, it kept pulling me in, and I ultimately connected with it on a deeper level in 2020, when I was looking for tools to help me feel safety within myself during a time when the world felt very unsafe. I had been feeling a lot of fear that wasn't always my own, and I knew I wanted to learn more about this modality because it had previously helped me get through an incredibly tumultuous transition period. My teacher, Erin Telford, hosted free weekly breathwork sessions on her Instagram Live during the month of March, when the COVID-19 pandemic had first kicked in, and these sessions reconnected me to the practice, which I had given up on just two years earlier. Later, Erin announced that she was offering a virtual training for breathwork facilitation in February of 2021, and I jumped at this opportunity, which I saw as a fast track to deeper inner healing.

During the training, I learned the fundamentals behind breathwork facilitation, as well as intuitive techniques such as tuning into a client's energy to sense imbalances. We split up into pairs to practice the exercises and tools, ending the weekend with a breathwork session offered by our partners. As I lay down on my couch, settling in, my partner started the playlist for the session, and with the trust we had built over the weekend in our exercises together, I found myself completely at ease as I started with the active breath.

I was open to whatever wanted to come up for healing, and after the first fifteen minutes of activation by whatever wanted to be released, I saw a scene play out in my mind's eye of the day that I'd found out lockdowns were first happening. After releasing the tears, pain, and trauma I'd been carrying in my body from the start of the pandemic, I felt an overwhelming sense of love and expansiveness unlike anything I'd ever previously experienced, except for when I'd been on MDMA.

I experienced the same feelings of pure love and oneness. I was hot and sweaty, and somehow the texture of my hair felt soothing to me. My whole body was vibrating. My partner reflected back to me that she saw my aura, or energy field, as rainbow colored, and that my guides were present; they were asking that I call on them more often for support.

Breathwork is a portal into these non-ordinary states, which are typically only accessed through substance use, but you have more control through breathwork than you do through drugs, without any adverse side effects. This makes breathwork the perfect tool for those who have experienced trauma, because it's safe enough to practice without being retraumatized—which often is not the case with drugs. In these non-ordinary states of consciousness, you can connect with different types of guides, like angels and star beings. You may recognize their energy as one of intense love and support.

I went on to be trained in levels two and three of breathwork facilitation with Erin's teacher, David Elliott. These levels involve energetic exchange and working with groups, respectively. I also learned how to combine essential oils and apply them on different areas of the body to amplify the healing effects by increasing receptivity to the benefits of breathwork. Each of these trainings made me a better guide and coach,

through accessing new levels of healing in my own practice.
Next, I began recognizing the healing power of plants too.

CHAPTER 23

Plants

The plants have enough spirit to transform
our limited vision.

—Rosemary Gladstar

"Help me out, I'm stuck down here and it smells disgusting!" I
yelled to my mamie, from five feet below her garden's surface.
I had tried to jump across her composting structure—a deep
cement well—where she turned all her vegetative debris into
new soil. Instead of landing safely on the other side, I had fallen
into the pile of decomposing fruit and vegetable remains.

I've been around plants from a young age because of
Mamie's love for gardening. Almost her entire backyard is a
garden, and she spent hours a day tending potatoes, rhubarb,
lettuce, sunflowers, green beans, tomatoes, mirabelles (French
yellow plums), squash, and herbs. When I visited her each
summer while I was growing up, I would help prepare meals
by snipping off the ends of green beans, a task I learned to love
after initially loathing it. Even though she now lives in the

city, she still has a sizable plot reminiscent of her old French countryside gardens. Being there, among her plants, brings me peace.

Likewise, when I was a child, I often spent hours outside in our sprawling backyard, playing in the sprinkler or finding hidden caves under the bushes or lying on a blanket under a giant pine tree and pretending I lived out there like the protagonist in *My Side of the Mountain*. I'd stay outside until dark, and when I'd look up at the stars, I'd feel incredibly safe, even though I had no physical structure around me, like a tent.

Smelling some delicious lilacs at Harvard University's Arnold Arboretum when I was about nine years old.

I also became intrigued by natural, plant-based products when I was around ten years old. One day, I came across *The Body Book*, by Anne Akers Johnson, which was filled with tantalizing at-home spa recipes, using natural ingredients for face masks, cleansers, foot soaks, spa water, and hair masks. I saved up my pocket money to purchase this thirty-dollar book, as this was a significant purchase for me at that age.

I invited my friend Cara to come over and try these recipes with me, and I'll never forget how we made an egg-based face mask, followed by a honey-almond face scrub, a witch hazel and rosewater toner, and facial steam using rosemary. All the while, we sipped spa water, using a recipe from this book that I still use to this day: sliced lemon and cucumber steeped in water for the day.

I found the way back to my inner child years later, in search of stillness and sanctuary, by using such all-natural ingredients as grated apples, milk, rosemary, and bananas. When I first stopped drinking in 2016, I explored natural remedies to work with the emotions I had suppressed for so long. Then, as I've mentioned earlier, I came across an opportunity to distribute essential oils in 2017.

The essential oil industry is unregulated, and a lot of ineffective products are available. There is a science to manufacturing oils so they'll do what they're intended to, and I found a company that was built on a scientific foundation. By partnering with growers all over the globe, who have been distilling essential oils for decades and over multiple generations of families, the company, dōTERRA, has discovered how to pinpoint the optimum time to harvest the plants so the aromatics can be captured in the distillation process.

The name dōTERRA means "of the earth" in Latin. The company offers an essential oils specialist certification that teaches the various distillation methods used to extract oil from plants. I took this certification course in 2020, where I also learned the chemistry behind the beneficial features of essential oils and which oils offer which benefits. For example, oils high in linalool, such as lavender and magnolia, are calming, whereas oils high in limonene, such as lemon and wild orange, are both uplifting and calming at the same time.

One of my favorite lessons about essential oils involves the jasmine plant. The company's jasmine oil is sourced from

Egypt, where the temperate climate produces a fragrant and delicate white flower that must be picked, and the oil extracted, right when it blooms to maintain its potency. Jasmine flowers bloom in the early morning before the sun rises, so they must be carefully harvested by hand before dawn, usually around two thirty in the morning, about six months after planting.

My discoveries about essential oils boosted all the other lessons I'd learned about healing and growth, and I knew that becoming a wellness advocate, or consultant, with dōTERRA in early 2018, made perfect sense. This time, it was a decision led by my soul, not my ego.

Essential oils all hold energy in their vibrations, which then help us integrate changes in our lives by providing the emotional vibrations we need to shift. Essential oils are also highly volatile, and the oils are fat soluble, so it takes just twenty-two seconds for the molecules to reach the brain, two minutes to reach the bloodstream, and then another twenty minutes to reach every cell in the body.

According to the book *Emotions and Essential Oils*, essential oils are considered to be forty to sixty times more potent than fresh herbs and work through five healing stages:[2]

> Stage One: Healing the Physical Body—The oils fight unfriendly microorganisms, balance body functions, raise the body's energetic vibration, and purify organs, glands, and body systems. At this stage, the oils move the body into a higher vibration.
>
> Stage Two: Healing the Heart—The oils process old feelings and release suppressed emotions like sadness, judgment, low self-worth,

---

2. *Emotions and Essential Oils: A Reference Guide for Emotional Healing*, 6th ed. (Salt Lake City: Enlighten Alternative Healing, 2017).

grief, and stagnant anger to create space for positive emotions. At this stage, the oils connect with the heart.

Stage Three: Releasing Limiting Beliefs—The oils shine a light on limiting beliefs and emotional patterns to allow you to see what's been hidden under the surface, so that trapped energy can be released. Then you get to choose the new and positive beliefs you'd like to replace them. This stage is for when deeply rooted and long-term beliefs in your subconscious come up for healing.

Stage Four: Spiritual Awareness and Connection—The oils wake you up to the love that is always around you in many forms. Stage four connects with your spiritual awareness.

Stage Five: Life's Purpose—The oils reveal your purpose and give you courage to take the path that's meant for you. This is for when you've cleared the detrimental patterns and stuck energy.

This healing process is similar to the coaching curriculum I now take my clients through. An important lesson I took away from this book was that essential oils—or any plant medicine, for that matter—don't do our emotional work for us. They facilitate it, and they are not meant to be relied on as the sole tool for healing. Otherwise, it's like using a substance outside ourselves to cling to, akin to turning to alcohol or weed to cope, which is why combining the oils with coaching, therapy, meditation, energy healing, breathwork, and personal development facilitates healing. These are the pathways to healing that essential oils can support.

Some of the oils that have helped me through challenging transitions have been rosemary, which is the oil of knowledge and transition, and Siberian fir, which is the oil of aging and perspective. Rosemary especially helps if you're having difficulty adjusting, by showing you it's safe to trust in a higher, more intelligent power than yourself, so you feel confident and assured during times of great change. Siberian fir helped me look honestly at my life choices and my legacy at a point when I was confused about the next steps in my career. This plant helped me let go of regrets and find the wisdom and purpose with each new chapter of my life.

Frankincense, the oil of truth, helped with grief surrounding my dad's death by creating a healthy attachment with the father figure and reminding me that I am loved and protected. It's a spiritual oil, perfect for meditation and prayer, that allows me to connect to God and my father, thereby clearing the dark emotions of grief.

One of my clients, Sara, found that a blend of lemongrass, Litsea, and rosemary helped her heal, alongside my coaching. She'd come to me for help with forgiveness and healing from past trauma related to her work experiences. After using the oil blend and completing forgiveness exercises—such as the Ho'oponopono practice, which involves a prayer for thanking the people who have hurt you, letting them know you forgive and love them, and letting them go—she was able to finally move forward and release her grievances. This opened her up to greater clarity, which helped her realize she needed to decide between a career that was more aligned with her high aspirations and her current job. After we worked together and she connected to her heart using the oils to support forgiveness and manifestation, she made her decision and successfully negotiated a promotion and raise that allowed her to remain with her current employer, something that she had secretly desired for years but that wasn't possible until this work together.

My love for plants has been rekindled and expanded to higher levels than ever before. Plants, just like humans and animals, have a consciousness, a spirit that resides within, and they are here to partner with us and help us transmute the challenges we go through, as our consciousness expands. They are also multidimensional, like us, and they impart the energetic qualities we need. In this sense, they are allies that we can turn to in our daily lives and during major life transitions. They can serve as supports for our bodies and souls by oxygenating and purifying the air in our homes, calming our nerves, and holding space for us in our most challenging moments. They also help us avoid toxins when we use them in place of products with synthetic fragrances.

When I started my podcast in 2020, I hadn't initially been planning to do so. It was meant to be a YouTube recording, but due to technological issues, it wound up being a podcast. Suddenly I found myself booking interviews months out with experts on plant healing and people who had created fulfillment in their work and life.

My guests have come on the podcast to talk about brain health with essential oils, healing with herbal loose-leaf tea, working with plants as allies for growth and abundance, speaking with plants, using flower essences to heal, therapeutic flower arranging, and so much more. Thanks to them, I've started working with plants (not *using* them; remember, they are allies) in my personal development. I ingest nonalcoholic flower essences daily; drink various loose-leaf teas, depending on my goals; bathe with flower petals and essential oils; and eat adaptogenic mushrooms, as well as the Ayurvedic herbs ashwagandha and brahmi. I enjoy a plant-based lifestyle in every sense of the meaning, starting with the food I eat, and this relationship with plants has put me on the fast track to joy, enlightenment, freedom, and peace. I have seen these effects in my clients, too, with one session in particular that will stay with me for a lifetime.

The virtual session started with my client, Melissa, sharing her intentions for healing. She wanted to feel connected to herself again after a recent move back home to Iowa had led her to feeling disconnected and depressed. She shared how ungrounded she felt, and in the cold winter climate, she felt cooped up at home and stuck in her head, unsure of her next steps. After Melissa shared her intentions for that particular session, I asked her to lie down, get comfortable, and drop into the present moment. I guided her through active breathing, and the deeper her breathing went, the more I could sense and see her sadness being slowly softened.

After a sudden release of tears, Melissa shared how she just realized how disconnected she had felt from nature and that she needed her plants. She suddenly got up from her bed in her room to hug all her houseplants, nearly crying in their leaves and smudging soil all over herself. Her breakdown had shown her how disconnected she had been from nature, and she needed to get closer to plants in the only way she could at that moment. She demonstrated our inherent relationship with plants and nature, which runs much deeper than it seems on the surface.

Find ways that you can weave plants into your lifestyle, a little at a time. Maybe you can create botanical art or choose loose-leaf teas as a beverage of choice. You might also try diffusing certified pure, therapeutic-grade essential oils before bed. Notice how the plants raise your vibration, imbuing emotions of peace, and reflect back to you the innate nature of continuous growth. Plants are here to love, guide, and heal you in a way that no other human or manmade tool can. Nurture this relationship with plants and see how much lighter and more expansive you can be. And how free.

CHAPTER 24

With New Eyes

If you believe it will work out, you'll see
opportunities. If you believe it won't, you will
see obstacles.

—Wayne Dyer

The whole point of working on yourself, healing your wounds, clearing your blocks, and upgrading your mindset is to set yourself free. Free from limitations, from pain. To feel whole as you are. To feel safe and seen in your relationships, to experience deeper intimacy and joy in them. It's to feel stability in yourself and be able to trust that you can handle whatever life throws your way. It's not only to make yourself better but to improve all the relationships you have in your life.

It starts with balancing your physical body, to house the ideal environment for your unfolding, like how I was led to stop drinking and adopt a vegan and nontoxic lifestyle. Your body has to be nourished first.

Wholeness is not all about collecting crystals, chanting in full moon circles, and going on spiritual retreats. While those aspects can be part of it, that's not the point. Yet, in today's world, people use spirituality to define themselves. This is just another trap of the ego. I did it too. When I first woke up, I thought I could only have spiritual people in my life because they would be the only ones able to understand me. Over time, I've learned that this could not be more false, and I've tossed away this dangerous, polarizing belief.

Not everyone in your life will have the same spiritual pursuits that you do, and by all means, it can be challenging to connect if you have different views. But they'll still be able to connect and understand you on a soul and heart level. Be sure that you do have connections in your life who share the same spiritual interests, but also balance this with people who aren't interested in this lifestyle too.

Waking up has brought me closer to myself, to my soul; life is about more than having a physical experience. Life starts to change when you connect your passions to your soul purpose. Your purpose creates that inner fire that truly sets your soul ablaze. Your soul is your inner powerhouse that can direct the flow of energy in your life. Simple as that. I believe the purpose of this experience on earth as a soul is to learn, to grow, and to love. When you clear out old stories and reclaim your narrative, you uncover your purpose and start to direct the flow of your life, instead of being directed. Working on yourself, through healing, learning, and working with a coach, healer, or therapist, simply puts you in the driver's seat of your life.

Your challenges in times of transition are to find the right tools that will shape you into the person you want to become and to take empowered action. I look back at how frustrated I was at all the different challenging transitions in my life, and I smile now in absolute awe and gratitude for how they unfolded. All to my benefit. I'm glad that the universe was in charge of the timeline, because I wouldn't be where I am without the process that was needed. After you've set your intentions, surrender your timeline to the universe. It will know better than you how much time and space you need to unfold.

Want to navigate your challenges smoothly and come out better on the other side? One way to do this instantly is by taking responsibility for every aspect of your life. You'll step out of victim mode, and that's when your mindset and self-worth will elevate your life. That's when you'll free yourself from the illusion that your external circumstances are controlling your life—the lie that keeps you stuck. To free myself from the sneaky victim mindset, I had to own how I show up in my life and understand that life is a mirror of what I'm feeling and believing inside. All my challenges, from being in places where I didn't feel I belonged, were leading me to a place of fully accepting myself for who I am, and not being apologetic in how I show up in the world. I saw how the work I did on myself, through my investments in coaching and healing, gave me a more free, expansive, and, honestly, pretty freaking awe-inspiring life. Transformation takes a decision to say yes to growth and support on that path.

Don't think this work is selfish either. When we each work on self-development and the shifting of consciousness, we are seeding the new earth, the next golden age. Healing ourselves means healing our ancestral lineage from the past and into the future. Healing our energy affects society's collective energy. It's not only about you or me. If we really start to think about it, healing actually ends up being selfless work.

By dedicating ourselves to cultivating the right mindset and seeking support from others who have done what we are aiming to do, we are connecting with like-minded people, including healers, thought leaders, and coaches. This collective effort will expand our lives and take us where we never thought it would be possible to go on our own.

Those challenging transitions we go through have the ability to soften us, open our hearts wide, make us more present, and allow us to empathize with others. In this world, it's so easy to close off a part of ourselves, and harden our hearts, to avoid feeling the inherent pain of being human. When we are open, and healing, we are able to meet people, heart to heart, where we once couldn't. The challenges we overcome reflect how we can serve others, whether in our careers or elsewhere.

I'm a fan of keeping things simple. You now understand how everything is energy and that influencing your mindset comes from influencing the energy of emotions and patterns in your subconscious. Using the breath in breathwork along with plants simply transfers high vibrational energy into your own energetic field, or aura. Plants have a divine intelligence we can work with to support ourselves in our healing and be in relationship with, just like people. The breath is a form of spiritual energy that can reset your patterns and stagnant energy. Connecting with your inner child, healing your ancestral patterns, developing your self-worth, knowing yourself, making aligned friendships, connecting with your creativity, and setting boundaries will allow you to access all parts of yourself, and therefore live intentionally.

Stay simple in your approach to wholeness and mastery. On the other side of introspection, intention, and resilience is your freedom. Freedom to show up as who you are, which gives others permission to do the same. Walking this path is not for the faint of heart; it's for the bold and brave. On the other side of healing, a surge of unencumbered creativity, connection, and clarity of purpose awaits you.

The challenges I went through led me home to myself and then on to help others. It took me years to get to this place of acceptance in this role, but I now see so clearly how I went through certain experiences, sometimes taking much longer than I wish they would have, all so that I could learn to overcome a multitude of challenges and show others how to do the same with ease. Most empathic people have the traits they do because they have been burned and want to give what they never received. Remember that giving love, support, a listening ear, and acceptance to others is in fact a way of also giving to yourself, perhaps even on behalf of the people who never gave this to you. My life experiences are what have made me into the wise, patient, present, and resilient woman that I am today.

The people who have helped me along the way gave me the permission to turn myself around and hold space for others so that they, too, can transform. It's a reciprocal energy, and I know from healing myself and carving my own path that it's for others' benefit too. I know that my experiences through grief, harassment, uncertainty, moving abroad, burnout, addiction, anxiety, depression, estrangement, and career pivots have helped me be able to relate and hold space for women going through the exact same transitions.

Your pain is the portal to your power and to the greatest version of yourself. When you view your challenges in this light, you build resilience and see that these moments in time are all for your benefit. The best question I love to ask myself when going through a challenge is this: *What is this trying to teach me?* When you reflect on that, you'll discover that there is always a lesson there for you, which you'll be able to integrate much more smoothly when you understand the purpose of the challenge.

Your pain is a blessing, meant to influence your behavior and help you make new choices that you wouldn't have been able to make without it. You can't hate the experiences that brought you to where you are now; accepting them and learning from them is how you alchemize the pain. These events in my life were leading me to find wholeness within, which was always present, but it had to be unearthed. Like me, you, too, can make the decision to look within, by committing to fully seeing and accepting all facets of yourself. You are not alone in this experience; seen and unseen forces are guiding you, if you choose to open yourself to them.

RECOMMENDED READING

Byrne, Rhonda. *The Secret*, 10th anniversary ed. New York: Atria Books/Beyond Words, 2006.

Cameron, Julia. *The Artist's Way*, 25th anniversary ed. New York: TarcherPerigee, 2016.

Covey, Stephen R. *The 7 Habits of Highly Effective People: Powerful Lessons in Personal Change*, 25th anniversary ed. New York: Simon & Schuster, 2013.

Craighead George, Jean. *My Side of the Mountain*, New York: Dutton Books, 1988.

Essential Emotions. *Essential Emotions: Your Guide to Process, Release, and Live Free.* Highland, UT: Essential Emotions, 2020.

Foundation for Inner Peace. *A Course in Miracles*, 3rd ed. Glen Allen, CA: Foundation for Inner Peace, 1975.

Hay, Louise. *You Can Heal Your Life*, illustrated ed. Carlsbad, CA: Hay House, 1984.

Hicks, Esther, and Jerry Hicks. *Ask and It Is Given: Learning to Manifest Your Desires.* Carlsbad, CA: Hay House, 2004.

King, Stephen. *On Writing: A Memoir of the Craft*, 1st ed. New York: Scribner, 2000.

Nelson, Bradley. *The Emotion Code: How to Release Your Trapped Emotions for Abundant Health, Love, and Happiness.* New York: St. Martin's Essentials, 2019.

Ruiz, Don Miguel. *The Four Agreements: A Practical Guide to Personal Freedom (A Toltec Wisdom Book)*. San Rafael, CA: Amber-Allen, 1997.

Waldman, Lara. *Money Manifestation Mastery*. London: New Generation, 2017.

Zinsser, William. *On Writing Well: The Classic Guide to Writing Nonfiction*, 30th anniversary ed. New York: Harper Perennial, 2016.

ABOUT THE AUTHOR

Author and podcast host at Guide to Wholeness, Emily Smith is the go-to spiritual coach who helps high-achieving women heal from their past so they can create fulfilling careers, starting with instilling self-confidence. With an extensive background in holistic living, Emily is trained in breathwork facilitation and is certified as an essential-oil specialist and an integrative life coach.

Emily coaches her female clients through major life transitions by providing space for them to navigate their emotions and rebuild their sense of worthiness and faith. Over the years, she has developed a unique methodology to release trapped emotions, combined with strategies to shift the subconscious mind, in order to fully embody life changes on a mind-body level. Her expertise has been featured in Bustle, Thrive Global, Thought Catalog, and *Authority Magazine*. She has been requested to speak at coveted stages, corporations, and international retreats. She connects with a wide audience across the world through her daily LinkedIn posts.

When she isn't connecting with her clients, Emily takes pleasure in traveling the world and experiencing different cultures, making new connections, discovering new spots in nature to hike with her rescue pup, and discussing astrology and the universe.

Printed in Great Britain
by Amazon